Conquer the World:
How to Overcome Insurmountable Obstacles – A Lesson from Scipio Africanus

Rowan X. Adler

Adler Horizons

www.rowanxadler.com

Introduction: Meet Scipio Africanus – Your Guide to Conquering Obstacles

When we think of ancient Rome, images of grandeur and invincibility often come to mind—armies clad in iron, conquering lands far and wide. Yet, Rome's history is also a tale of vulnerability, marked by moments of near destruction. One of the most perilous eras in Roman history came during the Second Punic War, when Hannibal Barca, a Carthaginian general of unmatched brilliance, marched his armies—including war elephants—over the Alps and into the heart of Italy. His genius threw Rome into chaos, leaving its citizens questioning whether the Republic could survive. It was in this dire moment of despair that a young man named Scipio Africanus began his extraordinary rise.

Scipio was no ordinary Roman. While many of his peers focused on surviving the crisis, Scipio set his sights higher: not just enduring Hannibal's onslaught, but outthinking and outlasting him. He didn't come from obscurity—he was the son of a respected Roman general—but his youth and relative inexperience made his achievements all the more remarkable. In a world dominated by older, seasoned commanders, Scipio stood out not only for his courage but for his willingness to embrace innovative strategies that defied Roman military tradition.

A Turning Point: The Boy Who Saved His Father

One of the earliest glimpses of Scipio's indomitable spirit occurred when he was just 17 years old. It was the Battle of Ticinus, a confrontation between Roman forces and Hannibal's army during the early stages of the war. Scipio's father, also named Publius, was commanding the Roman troops. Hannibal's cavalry launched a devastating attack, overwhelming the Roman forces. As the soldiers scattered in disarray, Publius lay wounded on the battlefield, surrounded by enemy cavalry.

It was here that young Scipio stepped forward. Rallying a small contingent of soldiers, he charged into the fray, fighting his way to his injured father. Against overwhelming odds, he managed to rescue him and lead the remaining troops to safety. This act wasn't just an act of filial loyalty—it was a defining moment of courage and quick thinking under pressure. For the men who witnessed it, Scipio was no longer a mere boy; he had proven himself as a leader, someone capable of turning the tide even in the bleakest circumstances.

This incident became a cornerstone of Scipio's legend. It demonstrated not only his bravery but his ability to act decisively in the face of chaos—an ability that would define his career and make him one of Rome's greatest generals.

A Leader Born in the Shadow of Hannibal

At the time of Scipio's emergence, Hannibal was the terror of Rome. Known for his audacious tactics and uncanny ability to outwit Roman generals, Hannibal seemed unstoppable. His victories at battles like Cannae—where the Roman army suffered one of the worst defeats in its history—left the Republic reeling. To ordinary Romans, Hannibal was a nightmare incarnate, a symbol of Carthaginian ingenuity and ruthlessness. To Scipio, however, Hannibal was a challenge—a mountain to climb rather than an insurmountable wall.

This determination to confront and overcome the seemingly invincible set Scipio apart. While others were paralysed by fear, Scipio began studying Hannibal's methods, seeking to understand his strengths and, more importantly, his weaknesses. It's no exaggeration to say that Scipio's ability to think like his enemy became one of his greatest strengths.

Scipio as a Metaphor for Perseverance

Scipio's life is more than a historical account of military campaigns—it's a metaphor for resilience, strategic thinking, and the power of innovation. He grew up in a world where the odds were stacked against Rome. Yet, instead of succumbing to despair, he adapted, learned, and ultimately overcame. His journey demonstrates a timeless truth: success isn't about having the perfect conditions or the easiest path. It's about finding ways to move forward, even when the terrain is rough and the obstacles seem insurmountable.

Consider Scipio's decision to take the war to Africa, a move that many in the Roman Senate viewed as reckless. It was bold, audacious, and risky—but it was also meticulously planned. Scipio understood that to defeat Hannibal, Rome couldn't remain on the defensive. This willingness to take calculated risks is a lesson that transcends time, offering inspiration to anyone facing daunting challenges, whether in their career, relationships, or personal growth.

A Promise to the Reader

This book is your guide to navigating your own challenges through the lens of Scipio's life. You don't need to command legions or face an invading army to apply his lessons. His strategies—courage in adversity, strategic thinking, adaptability, and the ability to inspire others—are just as relevant today as they were in ancient Rome.

Through Scipio's story, you'll discover practical tools and insights to overcome obstacles in your own life. Whether you're struggling with a demanding job, trying to master a difficult skill, or facing setbacks in your personal relationships, Scipio's journey provides a roadmap for turning adversity into opportunity.

The Battle of Zama: The Climactic Lesson

As we embark on this journey, it's worth keeping an eye on the destination: the Battle of Zama. This final confrontation between Scipio and Hannibal was the culmination of years of preparation, learning, and growth. It wasn't just a clash of armies—it was a battle of minds, a testament to Scipio's ability to outthink even the greatest military strategist of his age. Zama was Scipio's moment of triumph, and as you'll see, it holds lessons that can illuminate your own path to success.

So, as we delve into Scipio's life, remember: his story isn't just history. It's a blueprint for overcoming challenges, building resilience, and conquering the seemingly impossible. Like Scipio, you too can find ways to rise above the odds—and perhaps, one day, achieve a victory worthy of your own Zama.

The Book's Promise

Throughout history, humanity has sought guidance from its heroes—figures who overcame monumental challenges and left behind a legacy of wisdom. Scipio Africanus, one of Rome's greatest generals, embodies such a figure. His life is not just a tale of military conquest but a masterclass in navigating adversity, seizing opportunities, and inspiring others. This book promises to take the lessons from Scipio's extraordinary journey and apply them to the challenges of modern life, whether you're climbing the career ladder, recovering from personal setbacks, or struggling with seemingly insurmountable obstacles.

Scipio's strategies weren't just about outwitting his enemies—they were about outthinking his circumstances. When Rome was on the brink of collapse, he didn't merely react to crises; he reframed them as opportunities to innovate. He taught his soldiers, his allies, and even his rivals the power of courage, vision, and adaptability. These are lessons that transcend the battlefield, offering tools for today's readers to overcome their own struggles.

What makes this book different? It's not just a history lesson or a self-help manual. It's a fusion of both, providing readers with a lens to see their own lives through the timeless principles that made Scipio a legend. You'll learn how to approach challenges strategically, turn setbacks into springboards, and build the resilience needed to face life's most demanding trials. And it won't just be theory—we'll walk you through practical exercises and tools to help you integrate these lessons into your daily routine.

Preview: The Battle of Zama—Scipio's Defining Moment

Every great story needs a climax, a moment where everything the hero has learned is put to the test. For Scipio Africanus, that moment was the Battle of Zama. This decisive confrontation against Hannibal, his lifelong adversary, wasn't just a military engagement—it was the culmination of years of preparation, resilience, and strategic brilliance. Zama represents the ultimate expression of Scipio's principles and is the narrative thread tying this book together.

What made Zama so remarkable wasn't just Scipio's tactical genius; it was his ability to adapt, to learn from his enemy, and to execute a vision with precision. Hannibal had terrorised Rome for nearly two decades, and many considered him unbeatable. Scipio, however, saw the cracks in Hannibal's seemingly impenetrable armour. He didn't simply rely on brute force; he relied on insight and ingenuity. This battle serves as a metaphor for the struggles we face in our own lives—moments when we must confront our own "Hannibals" and rise to the occasion.

Zama teaches us that triumph is rarely the result of sheer determination alone. It's about preparation, learning from the past, and being willing to take calculated risks. As you'll see in this book, these principles are just as applicable to modern challenges—whether you're trying to overcome professional stagnation, rebuild after a failure, or master a skill that feels out of reach.

Themes to Guide Your Journey

As we explore Scipio's life, three core themes will emerge, each offering insights for your own challenges:

1. **Resilience**:
Resilience isn't about avoiding hardship—it's about enduring and adapting to it. Scipio grew up in the shadow of Rome's darkest hour, yet he used these early trials to cultivate an unshakable resolve. In this book, you'll learn how to build your own resilience,

using setbacks as opportunities for growth rather than reasons to give up.

2. **Strategy**:
Success often depends on the ability to think several steps ahead. Scipio's victories were rarely the result of brute force; they were the outcome of meticulous planning and creative problem-solving. Whether you're managing a complex project, resolving conflicts, or tackling a personal goal, this book will help you craft your own strategies for success.

3. **Leadership**:
Great leaders inspire others to rise above their limitations. Scipio's ability to motivate his troops and form crucial alliances was key to his success. In this book, we'll explore the qualities that make a leader effective—qualities you can apply not just in the workplace but in your relationships and community.

A Timeless Maxim: "Fortune Favours the Brave"

One of Scipio's defining traits was his willingness to take bold, calculated risks. Whether it was leading a daring campaign in Spain or deciding to invade Africa against the advice of many Roman senators, Scipio knew that great rewards often require great courage. His life echoes the timeless maxim: *Fortune favours the brave.*

This principle isn't about recklessness—it's about recognising when the stakes are worth the risk and preparing yourself to seize the moment. In this book, we'll examine how to cultivate the courage to make bold decisions in your own life, balancing audacity with careful planning. Whether you're considering a career change, starting a new venture, or stepping outside your comfort zone, you'll find actionable strategies to help you embrace bravery in the face of uncertainty.

What Awaits You

This book will guide you through Scipio's life, exploring his triumphs and tribulations as stepping stones to understanding how you, too, can conquer the obstacles in your path. Each chapter will delve into a different phase of Scipio's journey, pairing historical insights with modern psychology and practical exercises. You'll find yourself learning not just about Scipio, but about yourself—your potential, your strengths, and your capacity to overcome.

By the time you finish this book, you'll have a new perspective on the challenges you face, a toolkit of strategies to tackle them, and, most importantly, the belief that no obstacle is insurmountable. Like Scipio, you'll learn to see every challenge as an opportunity to rise to your own greatness.

So, are you ready to conquer your own Zama? Let's begin.

Chapter 1:

The Shadow of Hannibal – A Childhood in Crisis

To understand the man who would eventually bring Rome its salvation, we must first journey back to the years when Scipio Africanus was not yet a hero but a boy navigating one of the darkest periods in Roman history. Scipio was born into a world on the brink of collapse. The Second Punic War, a conflict between Rome and its ancient rival Carthage, raged with unrelenting ferocity, and at the centre of Rome's despair stood Hannibal Barca—a general so brilliant and audacious that he seemed invincible.

Hannibal's campaign in Italy, marked by one staggering victory after another, shattered Rome's confidence. By the time Scipio reached his late teens, the young Republic had endured a string of crushing defeats, the most infamous being the Battle of Cannae. This catastrophic encounter was not just a military loss; it was an existential crisis for Rome. For a boy like Scipio, growing up in such a climate of fear and uncertainty, the war must have seemed like a force of nature—unrelenting and impossible to control.

Witnessing Rome's Darkest Hour

Hannibal's invasion of Italy began with an audacious move: marching his army, including war elephants, over the Alps—a feat many thought impossible. From there, he carved a path of destruction through Italy, winning battles with a combination of cunning strategy and psychological warfare. He did not merely defeat Roman armies; he humiliated them. Hannibal's name became synonymous with terror, and stories of his ruthlessness spread like wildfire, leaving the Roman populace in a state of dread.

One of the defining moments of this era—and of Scipio's formative years—was the Battle of Cannae in 216 BCE. In this encounter, Hannibal encircled a much larger Roman army in a brilliant manoeuvre, annihilating it. Nearly 50,000 Roman soldiers were killed in a single day, with many of Rome's best commanders among the dead. The survivors were scattered, humiliated, and demoralised. Rome itself was left defenceless, its fields abandoned, its citizens paralysed by fear.

Imagine what it must have been like for a young Scipio to witness this. He wasn't yet a commander or even a soldier of note. He was a teenager, barely old enough to understand the complexities of war, but already living in its shadow. For him and his peers, Hannibal was not just an enemy; he was a living nightmare, a symbol of everything Rome could lose. Yet, while others despaired, Scipio was quietly observing, learning, and preparing for a future in which he might help turn the tide.

The Oath at Cannae

History tells us that in the aftermath of Cannae, Scipio and a close friend, Lucius Aemilius Paullus, swore an oath that would become legendary. In the face of Rome's devastation, they pledged to fight on, to resist the overwhelming despair that had gripped their city, and to dedicate their lives to Rome's survival and eventual victory. This moment, whether entirely factual or partly mythologised by later historians, captures the essence of Scipio's resilience and determination.

The significance of this oath goes beyond mere words. At a time when many Romans were considering desperate measures—including negotiating peace with Hannibal—Scipio's vow was an act of defiance. It was a refusal to accept defeat, a statement that even in the darkest hour, there was still hope. For Scipio, this wasn't just about personal ambition; it was about Rome itself—the idea that its values, its people, and its future were worth fighting for.

A Childhood in the Shadow of Fear

Growing up during Hannibal's invasion shaped Scipio in ways that would become evident throughout his life. Fear was a constant presence. Roman fields were burned, their towns pillaged, and their armies decimated. Refugees flooded into the city, bringing tales of horror and despair. Even within the walls of Rome, safety was not guaranteed. The spectre of Hannibal's army loomed so large that it was said Roman mothers would warn their children, *"Hannibal is at the gates,"* to keep them in line.

But fear can have two effects. For many, it paralyses. For others, it sharpens resolve. Scipio belonged to the latter category. Instead of succumbing to the terror of his times, he used it as fuel. He watched, he learned, and he dreamed of a future where Rome would no longer cower in Hannibal's shadow. This combination of observation and determination would become a hallmark of Scipio's approach to life. He wasn't just brave; he was thoughtful, deliberate, and endlessly optimistic, even when optimism seemed unwarranted.

Lessons from Cannae

The shadow of Hannibal taught Scipio lessons that would guide him throughout his life. First and foremost, it taught him the value of resilience. Rome did not fall after Cannae, despite the scale of the disaster. The Republic, battered and bleeding, found ways to rebuild, to adapt, and to endure. This ability to persist in the face of overwhelming odds became a cornerstone of Scipio's own philosophy.

Second, Scipio learned the importance of innovation. Traditional Roman tactics had failed against Hannibal's unorthodox strategies. If Rome was to survive, it needed leaders who could think differently, who could adapt and innovate. Scipio would become one of those leaders, breaking away from the rigid traditions of Roman warfare to craft strategies that mirrored Hannibal's ingenuity.

Finally, the era taught Scipio the necessity of hope. In the wake of Cannae, hope was in short supply, but it was the one thing Rome couldn't afford to lose. Scipio's oath to fight on was more than just a promise; it was a declaration that the Republic's spirit was unbroken.

Scipio's Foundations of Greatness

Scipio's childhood was not an easy one, but it was the perfect training ground for the man he would become. From a young age, he understood that greatness isn't born in times of peace and comfort; it's forged in the fires of adversity. He learned to face fear without flinching, to look beyond despair, and to find opportunity in chaos. These lessons weren't just theoretical—they were deeply personal, embedded in his very identity.

As we move forward in this book, you'll see how these early experiences shaped Scipio's approach to leadership, strategy, and life itself. His resilience in the face of Hannibal's terror, his willingness to adapt, and his unwavering belief in Rome's future are qualities that remain as relevant today as they were over two millennia ago. Whether you're navigating a career setback, rebuilding after a personal failure, or simply trying to stay hopeful in difficult times, Scipio's story offers a roadmap for turning adversity into opportunity.

Modern Parallel: Adversity and Resilience

Adversity has always been a universal experience, transcending time, geography, and culture. While the scale and specifics vary, the core truth remains the same: challenges, whether personal, societal, or global, shape who we are. For Scipio Africanus, growing up in the shadow of Hannibal's relentless campaign against Rome, adversity was an ever-present force. But adversity is not limited to the grand narratives of history—it is a constant in our modern lives as well. Whether it's the grinding effects of poverty, the pain of personal loss, or the structural barriers of systemic inequality, challenges are as relevant today as they were in Scipio's time.

Yet adversity is not inherently a sentence of despair. If navigated effectively, it can become the crucible where resilience is forged. In this way, Scipio's ability to rise above his circumstances is a mirror for our own potential to grow, adapt, and ultimately triumph.

Growing Up Amid Adversity

Consider the young person born into poverty, where every day is a test of endurance. Like Scipio facing Rome's darkest hour, they may feel overwhelmed by forces beyond their control—financial instability, limited opportunities, or an education system that seems stacked against them. The environment may seem relentlessly hostile, with little space for hope. And yet, as countless success stories have shown, it is often those who face such challenges who emerge with an unparalleled drive to succeed.

Personal loss, too, shapes us. Imagine a teenager losing a parent at a pivotal age, much like Scipio nearly lost his father on the battlefield. For many, this kind of emotional devastation can feel insurmountable. But in others, it sparks a deep wellspring of resilience, a determination to honour the memory of their loved one by living fully and striving for greatness.

Systemic challenges—racism, sexism, classism, and other entrenched inequalities—pose yet another layer of difficulty. For those who grow up under the weight of such barriers, the path forward is rarely straightforward. Success often requires navigating a world that is not designed with them in mind, a feat that demands both resilience and ingenuity.

In each of these examples, the parallels to Scipio's life are clear. Like Scipio, individuals facing adversity today must navigate a world fraught with uncertainty and obstacles. But just as Scipio refused to let the shadow of Hannibal define his future, modern individuals have the capacity to rise above their circumstances, armed with the resilience born from hardship.

The Science of Resilience: Post-Traumatic Growth

While adversity is an inescapable part of life, how we respond to it can vary greatly. For some, challenges lead to feelings of helplessness and despair. For others, adversity becomes a catalyst for growth—a phenomenon psychologists call *post-traumatic growth*. Unlike post-traumatic stress, which focuses on the negative impact of trauma, post-traumatic growth explores how individuals can emerge from hardship stronger, wiser, and more fulfilled.

Research on post-traumatic growth has identified several key areas where individuals often experience transformation:

- **Enhanced relationships**: People who endure hardship often develop a deeper appreciation for the support of friends and family.
- **New perspectives**: Adversity can shift priorities, helping individuals focus on what truly matters in life.
- **Inner strength**: Overcoming challenges fosters a sense of personal empowerment and resilience.
- **Greater appreciation for life**: Surviving hardship often brings a renewed sense of gratitude for life's simple joys.
- **Spiritual growth**: Many find a deeper connection to their faith or sense of purpose after enduring trials.

Scipio's life exemplifies this principle. His experiences of fear, loss, and uncertainty didn't defeat him—they transformed him. His ability to endure Rome's crises and emerge as a leader was not in spite of his hardships, but because of them. His resilience, creativity, and determination were all sharpened in the fires of adversity.

The Stress Inoculation Theory: Turning Challenges into Strengths

One of the most intriguing concepts in modern psychology is the **stress inoculation theory**, which suggests that exposure to manageable levels of stress can actually prepare individuals to handle greater challenges in the future. Just as a vaccine introduces a small dose of a virus to build immunity, manageable stress serves as training for the mind and body, teaching us how to adapt, problem-solve, and persevere.

Consider a child who faces mild setbacks early in life—perhaps losing a game, struggling with a difficult class, or learning to navigate disagreements with friends. While these experiences may feel uncomfortable in the moment, they build critical skills: emotional regulation, problem-solving, and a sense of self-efficacy. Over time, these small doses of stress inoculate the individual against larger challenges, creating a foundation of resilience.

In contrast, those who are shielded from all forms of stress may find themselves ill-equipped to handle adversity when it inevitably arises. Without the opportunity to learn coping mechanisms, they are more likely to feel overwhelmed by even minor setbacks. This is why modern parenting and education increasingly focus on teaching *grit*—the ability to persevere through difficulty—rather than avoiding challenges altogether.

Scipio's early years were, in many ways, a masterclass in stress inoculation. Growing up in a Rome under siege, witnessing Hannibal's devastating victories, and enduring personal and societal uncertainty all served to prepare him for the immense responsibilities he would later shoulder. By the time he took command of Roman forces in Spain, Scipio had already faced more stress and adversity than many seasoned commanders. He was ready—not because he had been spared from hardship, but because he had been tempered by it.

Lessons for Today

What can we take from Scipio's story and the science of resilience to apply to our own lives? The key is to view challenges not as roadblocks but as stepping stones. Here are some actionable steps for fostering resilience:

- **Reframe adversity**: Instead of asking, "Why is this happening to me?" ask, "What can I learn from this?"

- **Start small**: Seek out manageable challenges that stretch your abilities—whether it's learning a new skill, tackling a tough project, or stepping outside your comfort zone socially.
- **Cultivate self-awareness**: Reflect on past challenges and identify the skills they helped you develop. This builds confidence in your ability to handle future adversity.
- **Build a support network**: Resilience is often a team effort. Surround yourself with people who uplift and inspire you.
- **Celebrate progress**: Acknowledge your small victories—they're the building blocks of resilience.

Like Scipio, we all live in a world filled with uncertainty and obstacles. But by embracing adversity as a tool for growth, we can develop the resilience to not just survive, but thrive. Whether you're navigating personal loss, systemic challenges, or the stress of daily life, remember this: every hardship is an opportunity to become stronger. As Scipio himself showed, even in the darkest hour, greatness is within reach.

Bullet Points for Reflection

How Does Adversity Shape Character?

Adversity, while often unwelcome, is one of the greatest teachers in life. It forces us to confront our limitations, recalibrate our goals, and develop the skills necessary to navigate an unpredictable world. In Scipio Africanus's case, the challenges of his youth forged a leader of extraordinary resilience and ingenuity. Adversity compels us to grow in ways comfort never could—it chisels away complacency and strengthens resolve. But how exactly does it shape character?

- **Builds Emotional Fortitude**:

Adversity tests our ability to stay calm under pressure. It teaches us to regulate emotions, even in the face of fear or uncertainty, allowing us to make sound decisions when it matters most. Scipio's ability to lead his men despite the looming shadow of Hannibal exemplifies this emotional strength.

- **Encourages Adaptability**:

When faced with challenges, sticking rigidly to old methods often fails. Adversity pushes us to think creatively, adapt our strategies, and embrace innovation—key traits that allowed Scipio to outwit his Carthaginian rivals.

- **Fosters Empathy**:

Struggles create a deeper understanding of others' hardships. Leaders like Scipio, who faced adversity firsthand, often develop the ability to connect with and inspire their followers, making them more effective.

- **Refines Priorities**:

Hardship has a way of stripping life down to essentials. It helps us focus on what truly matters—whether that's family, personal goals, or a sense of duty.

As you reflect, ask yourself: How has adversity shaped you? What qualities has it drawn out in you that might have otherwise remained dormant?

Reflect on a Moment When You Faced a Significant Challenge

Think back to a timc when life tested you. Maybe it was the loss of a loved one, a career setback, or an academic hurdle that seemed insurmountable. Relive that moment—not to dwell on the pain, but to examine how you reacted. What emotions did you feel? What decisions did you make? Did you lean on others, or did you face it alone?

For example:

- Perhaps you lost a job unexpectedly and had to pivot to a new career path. How did that experience force you to grow? Did it uncover hidden strengths or spark a passion you hadn't explored before?

- Maybe you struggled with an academic subject you found daunting, only to discover that persistence and creative approaches eventually paid off.
- Or consider a personal loss that felt overwhelming at the time. How did you emerge from that experience, and how did it change your perspective on life and relationships?

These moments, though difficult, are often the ones that define us. As you reflect, try to focus not just on the pain or frustration, but on the strength and wisdom you gained from the experience.

Analyze How You Coped and What You Learned

The way we cope with challenges reveals a lot about who we are—and who we're becoming. Did you approach your challenge with determination and resourcefulness, or did you struggle to find your footing? Either way, there's value in examining your response.

- **Coping Mechanisms**:

What tools or strategies did you use to get through? Did you rely on problem-solving, seek help from others, or lean on personal rituals like journaling or exercise? Identifying what worked for you can help you build a toolkit for future challenges.

- **Lessons Learned**:

Every hardship carries a lesson. Did you learn the importance of patience, the value of asking for help, or the necessity of planning ahead? Perhaps you discovered an inner strength you didn't know you had.

- **Growth Areas**:

Adversity also highlights areas where we can improve. Were there moments where fear or frustration held you back? Did you procrastinate, avoid confrontation, or let self-doubt creep in? Recognising these patterns is the first step to overcoming them in the future.

Practical Exercise: Write a Resilience Timeline

Now that you've reflected on your challenges, it's time to map them out visually. A resilience timeline allows you to see your growth over time and identify the pivotal moments that shaped you. Follow these steps:

1. **Divide Your Life into Key Phases**:

Think about your life in chapters—childhood, adolescence, early career, recent years. Label these phases on a timeline.

2. **Plot Major Challenges**:

Mark the significant challenges you faced during each phase. These might include:

- Personal losses, like the death of a loved one.
- Professional setbacks, such as losing a job or facing rejection.
- Moments of self-doubt, failure, or fear.

3. **Identify Turning Points**:

For each challenge, note the moment when things began to change—when you found a solution, shifted your mindset, or received help.

4. **Highlight Skills Gained**:

Next to each challenge, write down what it taught you. For example:

- *Coping with grief* taught me the importance of cherishing relationships.
- *Overcoming academic failure* taught me perseverance and creative problem-solving.
- *Navigating a career setback* taught me adaptability and the value of seeking mentorship.

5. **Celebrate Your Progress**:

Look at the completed timeline and take pride in how far you've come. Each point on the timeline represents a victory, no matter how small.

6. **Optional Reflection**:

Write a brief summary of what your timeline reveals about your resilience. What patterns do you notice? How have you changed over time? Which skills or traits keep reappearing as your greatest strengths?

Closing Thought

Life rarely spares us from adversity, but it is through these trials that we discover our true potential. Just as Scipio Africanus emerged from his youth shaped by the hardships of Rome's darkest days, so too can we use our own challenges to forge resilience and strength. By reflecting on the past and recognising the skills we've gained, we can prepare ourselves to face the future with confidence and courage. Your resilience timeline isn't just a record of your past—it's a map for navigating what lies ahead.

Chapter 2:

Leading by Example – The Siege of New Carthage

Great leaders are forged in moments of crisis, and few moments are as electrifying as the Siege of New Carthage. For Scipio Africanus, this campaign was more than a military operation—it was a defining moment in his rise as a leader. It demonstrated his ability to think strategically, inspire loyalty, and take bold action, even against daunting odds. At just 25 years old, Scipio was tasked with leading Roman forces in Spain, a mission fraught with risk but ripe with opportunity. His success at New Carthage would solidify his reputation as a commander capable of not only winning battles but also winning the hearts and minds of his troops.

A City of Strategic Importance

New Carthage, or *Carthago Nova* as it was known, was the jewel of the Carthaginian holdings in Spain. Its location on the Mediterranean coast made it a critical hub for trade and military logistics. The city's wealth, natural harbour, and defences made it a prize that any army would covet. For Scipio, capturing New Carthage wasn't just a tactical objective—it was a statement of intent. By seizing this stronghold, he could cut off Carthaginian supply lines and establish a Roman foothold in Spain, turning the tide of the war.

But taking the city was no small feat. New Carthage was a fortress, heavily fortified on three sides by walls and on the fourth by the sea. The Carthaginians believed their defences were impenetrable, particularly the shallow lagoon to the north, which they assumed no army would dare to cross. It was precisely this assumption that Scipio turned to his advantage.

Strategic Brilliance: The Attack Through the Lagoon

Before launching his assault, Scipio spent days studying the city's geography and defences. Where others saw obstacles, he saw opportunities. The lagoon, dismissed by the Carthaginians as a natural barrier, became the cornerstone of his plan. Scipio noticed that the tides in the lagoon receded at specific times, leaving a narrow window during which his troops could cross on foot.

Timing his attack with the low tide, Scipio ordered a contingent of soldiers to advance through the lagoon under cover of darkness. As dawn broke, the Carthaginians were taken by complete surprise. While they scrambled to defend the walls, Scipio launched a simultaneous assault on the city's main gate, dividing their forces and sowing chaos. His troops breached the defences, and within hours, New Carthage fell into Roman hands.

This victory wasn't just a display of tactical ingenuity; it was a psychological blow to the Carthaginians. Their stronghold, believed to be impregnable, had fallen in a single day. Scipio's ability to outthink his enemies and exploit their complacency would become a hallmark of his leadership style.

Leading from the Front

Scipio's success at New Carthage wasn't just a result of clever strategy—it was a testament to his leadership. Unlike some commanders who directed battles from a safe distance, Scipio led his men from the front. He wasn't content to issue orders and wait for the outcome; he fought alongside his troops, sharing their risks and triumphs.

This willingness to put himself in harm's way inspired a deep sense of loyalty among his soldiers. They saw in Scipio not just a commander but a leader who was willing to shoulder the same burdens they carried. His courage under fire, combined with his sharp mind, made him a figure they were eager to follow.

A Commander Crowned by His Troops

After the victory at New Carthage, Scipio's soldiers bestowed upon him the title of *Imperator*, a term reserved for commanders who had earned the respect and admiration of their troops through extraordinary achievements. This was no ceremonial gesture—it was a spontaneous declaration of loyalty and gratitude from the men who had fought under his command.

For Scipio, this title carried immense significance. It wasn't granted by the Roman Senate or decreed by tradition; it came directly from the people whose lives depended on his decisions. It was a reflection of the bond he had forged with his soldiers, a bond built on mutual respect, shared hardships, and a common purpose.

A Commander's Integrity: The Chivalrous Treatment of a Captive

The siege and capture of Carthago Nova marked a defining moment in both Rome's campaign and the legacy of its young commander, Scipio Africanus. Victory was assured, and as spoils of war were tallied and prisoners gathered, the atmosphere buzzed with triumph. Among the captives brought before Scipio was a young woman of extraordinary beauty. Unlike the other prisoners, she was presented not as an ordinary captive but as a trophy—a reward deemed worthy of a conquering hero.

Scipio's officers expected him to claim his prize without hesitation. This was, after all, the norm in the brutal theatres of ancient warfare. But as the woman stood before him, silent and trembling, Scipio raised a hand to halt proceedings. His question surprised everyone: "Who is this woman?"

His tone wasn't one of indulgence or curiosity—it was deliberate. He wanted her story. His officers exchanged glances, momentarily confused. In their eyes, her background mattered little. But for Scipio, it mattered entirely.

When Scipio learned she was betrothed to a nobleman from a local tribe, he made a decision that silenced the room. Rather than keeping her as a possession or bartering her for political gain, he ordered her immediate release. More than that, he summoned her fiancé, a man of standing in the local community. To ensure the young woman's dignity was preserved, Scipio not only reunited the couple but also provided an escort and gifts as a gesture of goodwill.

The reaction among his men was palpable. Some were awed, others confused, and a few muttered their disapproval—what leader gives away what is his by right? But Scipio's reasoning was clear: to win the loyalty of the people, Rome needed more than military might—it needed trust and respect.

The Ripple Effect of Honour

This single act rippled far beyond the gates of Carthago Nova. The young woman's family and tribe were overwhelmed with gratitude, pledging their support to Scipio. Word of his fairness spread quickly, painting him not just as a conqueror but as a leader of extraordinary integrity. Even those who opposed Rome began to see Scipio in a different light—not as a typical invader but as a man who valued honour above conquest.

For his troops, the gesture carried its own weight. They admired Scipio not just for his tactical genius but for the moral compass that guided his decisions. In a world where leaders often took what they could simply because they could, Scipio's actions set him apart. He became not just a commander, but a symbol of what leadership could and should be.

Leadership Lessons from Scipio's Chivalry

This moment is more than an anecdote—it is a timeless lesson in the power of integrity. Scipio's actions weren't solely driven by kindness; they were a masterstroke of diplomacy. By showing respect for the humanity of one captive, he achieved more than he could have through brute force or manipulation. His choice secured loyalty, built trust, and bolstered his reputation among both allies and enemies.

For modern readers, the takeaway is clear: **integrity is not weakness—it is strength.** Leaders who act with fairness and empathy inspire deeper loyalty than those who rule by fear or force. Small acts of honour can resonate far beyond the moment, shaping how others perceive you and how they respond to your leadership.

Making Integrity Relatable

Imagine a modern workplace scenario: a junior employee makes a critical mistake. A leader could choose to publicly reprimand them, asserting dominance and control. Alternatively, the leader could take a private, constructive approach—addressing the issue calmly, offering guidance, and giving the employee a chance to redeem themselves. This act of understanding, while seemingly minor, builds trust and motivates the employee to improve.

Similarly, Scipio's decision to release the young woman not only preserved his personal integrity but amplified his influence. His troops followed him not only for his victories but because he exemplified the values they respected.

Integrity as a Tactic

Scipio's treatment of the young woman demonstrates a truth often overlooked: compassion is a strategic asset. In environments dominated by power and self-interest, acts of fairness and humanity can wield immense influence. Scipio showed that success is not about taking everything by force—it's about building a foundation of trust, respect, and credibility.

As you navigate your own challenges—whether at work, in relationships, or in personal pursuits—consider how moments of integrity can shape your path. The choices you make, especially when no one is watching, define not only your character but also how others perceive and support you.

Just as Scipio earned loyalty and admiration through his actions, you too can use integrity as a tool for lasting impact. In the words of Scipio himself:

"The best victories are not those fought with swords but those won with character."

Lessons from New Carthage: The Power of Leadership

Scipio's victory at New Carthage offers timeless lessons for modern leadership. Whether you're leading a team at work, guiding a community project, or navigating personal challenges, his example provides a blueprint for success:

1. **Find Opportunity in Obstacles**:

Scipio's decision to exploit the lagoon showed his ability to think creatively and turn a perceived weakness into a strength. When faced with challenges, consider the resources and opportunities others might overlook.

2. **Lead by Example**:

Scipio's presence on the front lines demonstrated his commitment to his troops. True leaders inspire trust and loyalty by sharing in the risks and rewards of their team's efforts.

3. **Integrity as a Leadership Tool**:

Scipio's treatment of the young captive wasn't just an act of kindness; it was a strategic move that built trust and goodwill. In any leadership role—whether at work, in your community, or even within your family—integrity is a currency that pays dividends.

4. **Inspire Loyalty Through Action**:

Titles like *Imperator* aren't earned through words—they're earned through deeds. Scipio's soldiers followed him not because they were ordered to, but because he had earned their respect through his actions.

5. **Seize the Moment**:

Scipio's timing of the attack during low tide was a masterstroke. In life, as in war, timing can make the difference between success and failure. Recognise the moments when the tide is in your favour and act decisively.

The Legacy of New Carthage

The capture of New Carthage wasn't just a military victory—it was a turning point in the Second Punic War. It demonstrated to Rome that Hannibal wasn't invincible, that the Carthaginians could be defeated through ingenuity and determination. For Scipio, it marked the beginning of his rise as a leader who could inspire and innovate, qualities that would define his career.

As we reflect on Scipio's triumph, it's worth considering how his example applies to our own lives. What challenges are you facing that seem insurmountable? What opportunities are hidden in the obstacles before you? And how can you lead others—whether at work, in your community, or in your family—with the courage and creativity that Scipio displayed?

The lessons of New Carthage remind us that leadership is not about having all the answers but about asking the right questions, taking calculated risks, and earning the trust of those you lead. Like Scipio, we all have the potential to rise through challenges and leave a legacy of innovation and inspiration.

Modern Parallel: Leadership in Everyday Life

Leadership is often romanticised as a grand, heroic endeavour—leading armies into battle, directing massive organisations, or creating global movements. But in reality, leadership takes place every day, in the small but significant interactions we have with the people around us. Whether you're managing a team at work, raising a family, or contributing to your community, you are constantly influencing those around you. The question is: what kind of influence are you exerting?

Scipio Africanus' leadership at New Carthage offers timeless lessons for these everyday scenarios. His ability to inspire his soldiers, think creatively, and lead from the front wasn't just about military strategy—it was about setting an example. By modelling the behaviour he wanted to see in his troops, Scipio demonstrated that great leadership begins with self-awareness and authenticity.

Leadership in Team Settings: Scipio's Integrity in Action

Whether you're at the helm of a corporate project or coordinating a neighbourhood initiative, leading a team requires more than just giving orders. Effective leaders understand the dynamics of their group and adapt their approach to suit the needs of their people. Just as Scipio Africanus demonstrated integrity and fairness alongside tactical brilliance, today's leaders can draw inspiration from his example. Let's explore how Scipio's leadership lessons translate to three common team settings:

1. The Workplace

Imagine managing a team under a tight deadline. Morale is low, and tensions are running high. You could pile on pressure, demanding results, or you could take a page from Scipio's book and lead by example. Roll up your sleeves and tackle a particularly challenging task alongside your team. This not only lightens their load but also demonstrates solidarity.

Scipio's actions during the siege of New Carthage exemplify this principle. When faced with a difficult assault, he didn't just direct his troops from safety—he fought alongside them. His willingness to share the risks and burdens earned him not just their obedience but their unwavering loyalty. Similarly, showing integrity in the workplace—by addressing concerns fairly or treating employees with respect—can build trust and inspire effort.

2. The Family

Leadership in the family setting often revolves around setting an example for others, whether it's children, partners, or relatives. Harmony starts with modelling the behaviour you wish to see. If you want honesty, kindness, or patience in your household, demonstrate those traits first.

Scipio's integrity extended beyond the battlefield. His treatment of the young woman at New Carthage—returning her to her fiancé unharmed—was a powerful act of respect and fairness. This decision didn't just reflect his values but set an example for his soldiers. Similarly, treating family members with patience and understanding can set the tone for how they interact with one another, fostering a culture of mutual respect.

3. The Community

Leadership in a community context might involve organising a local event, spearheading a volunteer initiative, or advocating for a cause. The most effective leaders are those who demonstrate commitment, authenticity, and fairness—qualities Scipio embodied.

After his soldiers declared him *Imperator* (commander), it wasn't just because of his strategic victories. Scipio had earned their respect through actions that reflected his character. Likewise, community leaders can build trust by consistently showing up, listening to others, and following through on their promises. For example, a local leader who treats all voices equally and acts with integrity—like Scipio—can unite people and inspire collective action.

Inspiring Others Through Modelling Behaviour

One of the simplest yet most powerful forms of leadership is leading by example. People are far more likely to follow someone who embodies the values they espouse. Scipio didn't demand courage from his troops while sitting safely in a tent—he fought alongside them, demonstrating the same bravery he expected from others. His treatment of allies and captives alike reflected his principles, showing that leadership is as much about actions as it is about strategy.

This principle applies to any setting where leadership is needed:

- **At Work**: If you want your team to meet deadlines, be punctual and prepared yourself. If you expect clear communication, model clarity and respect in your interactions.
- **In the Family**: Want your children to be honest? Demonstrate honesty in your actions. Value empathy? Show them what it looks like in practice.
- **In the Community**: Advocating for change? Make sure your actions reflect the values you're promoting. Leading a charity drive? Contribute your time or resources first before asking others to do the same.

By leading with integrity, you build trust and inspire those around you to rise to the occasion. Just as Scipio's example rallied his men and earned him enduring loyalty, your actions can have a profound impact on the teams, families, and communities you lead. True leadership, after all, is about practising what you preach.

Science Insight: The Psychology of Effective Leadership

Modern psychology has uncovered the traits that make leaders not only effective but also deeply trusted. Research consistently highlights two key qualities: **authenticity** and **vulnerability**.

1. **Authenticity**:

Authentic leaders are those who are true to their values and consistent in their actions. They don't pretend to be something they're not, and they don't demand behaviour from others that they wouldn't exhibit themselves. Authenticity fosters trust because it eliminates the disconnect between words and actions. When Scipio led his troops through the siege, his authenticity was on full display—he wasn't above his men; he was one of them.

2. **Vulnerability**:

While traditional notions of leadership often emphasise strength and infallibility, research shows that vulnerability is a crucial component of trust. Leaders who admit their mistakes, acknowledge their limitations, and show their human side are more relatable and approachable. Vulnerability doesn't mean weakness; it means recognising that no one has all the answers. By being open about your own challenges, you create an environment where others feel safe to share their ideas and concerns.

This combination of authenticity and vulnerability creates a foundation for effective leadership in any setting. It's not about being perfect—it's about being real.

Practical Exercise: Refining Your Leadership Style

To apply these lessons in your own life, take a moment to reflect on your leadership style and set actionable goals for improvement.

1. **Assess Your Leadership Style**:

Take stock of how you typically lead in different settings. Are you:

- **Directive**: Do you prefer to take charge and make decisions unilaterally?
- **Supportive**: Do you focus on empowering others and providing guidance?
- **Collaborative**: Do you prioritise teamwork and shared decision-making?

Each style has its strengths, but effective leaders know when to adapt their approach based on the situation and the people they're leading.

2. **Identify an Area for Growth**:

Choose one aspect of your leadership style to work on. For example:

- If you're directive, focus on listening more and involving others in decision-making.
- If you're supportive, challenge yourself to step into a more assertive role when necessary.
- If you're collaborative, ensure that consensus doesn't come at the expense of decisive action.

3. **Set a Goal to Model Positive Behaviour**:

Over the next week, identify one behaviour you'd like to model for your team, family, or community. For example:

- At work: Show punctuality by arriving early to meetings.
- At home: Demonstrate patience during difficult conversations.
- In your community: Take the lead on a task that others are hesitant to tackle.

4. **Track Your Progress**:

Keep a journal of your efforts throughout the week. Note:

- The specific actions you took to model positive behaviour.
- The reactions of those around you.
- Any changes you observed in the group dynamic.

5. **Reflect and Adjust**:

At the end of the week, review your journal. What worked well? What could you improve? Use these insights to refine your leadership approach moving forward.

Closing Thought: Leadership as a Lifelong Journey

Leadership is not about authority or titles—it's about influence and example. Scipio Africanus earned the loyalty of his troops not because he demanded it but because he deserved it. By leading from the front, modelling courage and integrity, and adapting his strategies to meet the moment, he inspired others to believe in his vision.

You don't need a battlefield to practise these principles. Whether you're mentoring a colleague, guiding your children, or organising a community effort, the essence of leadership remains the same. Be authentic, be vulnerable, and above all, lead by example. The people around you are watching—show them the kind of leader you can be.

Chapter 3:

The Turning Tide – Baecula and Ilipa

The campaign in Spain marked a pivotal chapter in the rise of Scipio Africanus, demonstrating his unparalleled ability to adapt, innovate, and seize the initiative. The *Battle of Baecula* (208 BC) and the *Battle of Ilipa* (206 BC) were far more than military victories—they were transformative moments that reshaped the course of the Second Punic War and solidified Rome's dominance in the region. These battles revealed Scipio's evolution from a promising young commander to a master strategist, shifting the tide of the war from defense to proactive offense.

The Battle of Baecula (208 BC)

Scipio's Assessment of Hasdrubal Barca

Scipio faced a formidable challenge in Hasdrubal Barca, the brother of Hannibal and a skilled Carthaginian commander. After his defeat at New Carthage, Hasdrubal sought to regroup and retreat northward to join forces with Hannibal in Italy. Scipio, however, anticipated his movements and resolved to intercept him before he could pose a greater threat.

- **Strategic Foresight**:

Scipio's ability to read his opponent's intentions was critical. He identified Baecula, a rugged location along Hasdrubal's expected route, as the perfect ambush site. Scipio's understanding of timing and geography allowed him to turn Hasdrubal's retreat into a vulnerable moment.

Terrain Advantage

Baecula was defined by steep slopes and rough terrain that would typically favour the defender. Yet Scipio saw an opportunity where others might have hesitated. By taking the high ground and leveraging the element of surprise, he transformed the Carthaginians' defensive advantage into their undoing.

- **High-Ground Maneuvering**:

Scipio positioned his forces on the ridges surrounding Hasdrubal's camp, effectively boxing in the Carthaginian army. His understanding of the terrain allowed him to outflank the enemy and catch them off-guard.

Unconventional Tactics

Rather than launching a predictable frontal assault, Scipio divided his army into multiple units, each tasked with a specific role in the ambush.

- **Flanking Forces**:

Two Roman contingents attacked Hasdrubal's rear and flanks, creating confusion and cutting off retreat paths. Meanwhile, the main force engaged the Carthaginians head-on, pinning them in place and preventing an organised defence.

- **Chaos and Confusion**:

This multi-pronged assault shattered Hasdrubal's formation, leaving his troops demoralised and vulnerable. The Carthaginian camp fell into disarray as Roman soldiers overran their positions.

Victory and Consequences

The *Battle of Baecula* was a decisive Roman victory that not only weakened Hasdrubal's forces but also disrupted his plans to reinforce Hannibal.

- **Strategic Impact**:

Although Hasdrubal managed to escape with a portion of his army, his remaining forces were significantly diminished. The loss undermined Carthaginian morale and resources, giving Rome a crucial advantage in Spain.

- **Prelude to Greater Battles**:

This victory set the stage for Scipio's next campaign, establishing him as a commander capable of turning defensive situations into offensive opportunities.

The Battle of Ilipa (206 BC)

Scipio's Bold Strategy

Two years after Baecula, Scipio faced an even larger Carthaginian force at Ilipa, led by Mago and Hasdrubal Gisco. Outnumbered and facing an enemy entrenched in traditional battle tactics, Scipio devised a plan that would outwit his opponents and decisively end Carthaginian dominance in Spain.

- **Deceptive Preparations**:

For several days leading up to the battle, Scipio used skirmishes to feign a predictable Roman formation. By mimicking standard deployments, he lulled the Carthaginians into a false sense of security.

- **Psychological Warfare**:

These manoeuvres not only misled the Carthaginians but also gave Roman troops the confidence to execute the bold plan that Scipio had in store.

Surprise Deployment

On the morning of the battle, Scipio revealed his true strategy—a radical reversal of his usual tactics.

- **Reinforced Flanks**:

Scipio placed his strongest troops, including his veteran legionaries, on the flanks, while weaker units held the centre. This formation defied Roman convention, designed specifically to exploit Carthaginian expectations.

- **Encirclement**:

As the Carthaginians concentrated their efforts on breaking through the Roman centre, Scipio's flanking units encircled them. Trapped and outmaneuvered, the Carthaginians found themselves overwhelmed.

A Crushing Blow

The *Battle of Ilipa* was a masterpiece of military strategy, resulting in a comprehensive Roman victory.

- **End of Carthaginian Influence in Spain**:

The defeat forced the Carthaginians to abandon Spain entirely, marking a decisive shift in the Second Punic War.

- **Legacy of Innovation**:

Military historians regard Ilipa as one of the most brilliant tactical victories of antiquity, cementing Scipio's reputation as a master strategist.

Themes and Lessons for Chapter 3

1. Strategic Thinking

- **Scipio's Example**:

Both Baecula and Ilipa highlight Scipio's ability to think several steps ahead, turning his enemies' strengths into weaknesses.

- **Modern Parallel**:

Strategic thinking in life or work involves anticipating challenges and creating proactive plans. For example:

  - In business, this might mean forecasting market trends to stay ahead of competitors.
  - In personal life, it could involve planning your education or career path with a clear long-term goal in mind.

2. Adaptability

- **Scipio's Flexibility**:

His willingness to abandon traditional tactics and embrace innovative solutions was key to his success.

- **Modern Parallel**:

Life often throws curveballs. Whether it's a sudden career shift or unexpected personal challenges, adaptability allows you to pivot and thrive.

Action

Scipio's Bold Moves:

The ambush at Baecula and the flanking strategy at Ilipa required confidence and calculated risk-taking.

- **Modern Parallel**:

Bold decisions—such as pursuing a new opportunity or confronting a difficult issue—are often necessary for growth and success.

4. Turning Points

- **Historical Significance**:

These battles marked a shift in the Second Punic War, transitioning Rome from a reactive to a proactive stance.

- **Modern Parallel**:

Recognising and seizing pivotal moments in your life can lead to transformative outcomes. For example:

  - Choosing to change careers despite initial uncertainty.
  - Taking a leadership role during a critical project.

Closing Thought: Scipio's Legacy in Spain

The *Battles of Baecula* and *Ilipa* were not just milestones in Scipio Africanus's career—they were turning points in the history of Rome. His ability to outthink and outmaneuver his enemies set a new standard for military leadership and demonstrated the transformative power of strategic vision, adaptability, and decisive action.

As you face your own challenges, remember Scipio's example. Every obstacle is an opportunity to think creatively, act boldly, and turn the tide in your favour. Whether your battlefield is the boardroom, the classroom, or your personal life, your victories are waiting to be claimed. Like Scipio, you have the power to shape your destiny—one battle at a time.

Themes and Lessons

The Turning Tide – Baecula and Ilipa

The victories at Baecula and Ilipa were more than tactical triumphs; they encapsulated timeless lessons in strategy, adaptability, and decisive action. These battles revealed Scipio Africanus as a leader who understood the value of foresight, the necessity of flexibility, and the importance of seizing pivotal moments. The themes drawn from his actions resonate powerfully with challenges we face in modern life, from navigating careers to fostering personal growth.

---

1. Strategic Thinking: The Power of Long-Term Planning

Scipio's Approach

Scipio Africanus was not a commander who focused solely on the immediate battlefield; he played the long game. At Baecula, he weakened Hasdrubal's forces to ensure they couldn't join Hannibal in Italy, effectively isolating Carthaginian strength. At Ilipa, he went further, dismantling Carthage's foothold in Spain entirely. These victories weren't just about winning battles—they were carefully orchestrated steps toward winning the war.

- **Anticipating Broader Implications**:

Scipio understood that every move was a piece of a larger puzzle. Each victory needed to serve a greater strategic goal, paving the way for Rome's eventual dominance.

Modern Parallel

Long-term success in life requires similar foresight. Whether in your career or personal endeavours, thinking several steps ahead can transform incremental efforts into significant achievements.

- **Professional**:
  - Plan your career with a clear end goal in mind. Anticipate industry trends, skill demands, and potential shifts in your field. For example, if technology is reshaping your industry, start upskilling now to remain competitive.
  - Build a network of mentors and peers who can support your growth.
- **Personal**:
  - Focus on developing relationships and skills today that align with your future aspirations. For example, nurturing a hobby like writing now might lay the foundation for a future creative career.

---

2. Adaptability: Flexibility in Changing Conditions

Scipio's Example

Adaptability was one of Scipio's defining traits. At Baecula, he exploited the rugged terrain to outmaneuver Hasdrubal, turning a defensive landscape into an offensive advantage. At Ilipa, he shattered expectations by deploying his strongest units on the flanks, abandoning conventional Roman tactics to achieve a decisive encirclement.

- **Using What's Available**:

Scipio didn't fight battles based on ideal conditions; he thrived in the reality of what he faced. His ability to pivot mid-campaign and innovate under pressure proved critical to his success.

Modern Parallel

Life rarely goes according to plan. Adaptability enables you to pivot, adjust, and find solutions in the face of unexpected challenges.

- **Professional**:
    - When a project encounters setbacks, don't double down on a failing approach. Assess the situation, reallocate resources, and consider alternative strategies.
    - For example, if a business plan isn't yielding results, adapting to new market data or consumer feedback can mean the difference between stagnation and growth.
- **Personal**:
    - Relationships, like battles, require flexibility. Whether it's adjusting to a partner's changing needs or navigating unexpected life events, adaptability helps relationships thrive.
    - For example, a family relocation might initially seem disruptive, but reframing it as an opportunity for new experiences can shift the narrative.

---

3. Decisive Action: The Courage to Take Risks

Scipio's Boldness

The ambush at Baecula and the deceptive deployment at Ilipa weren't just brilliant—they were audacious. Scipio's willingness to take calculated risks, even against larger forces, showcased his confidence and courage.

- **Calculated Risks**:

At Ilipa, his reversal of Roman battle formations was a gamble that required unwavering commitment. His belief in his strategy and his troops allowed him to execute bold moves with precision.

Modern Parallel

Success often demands stepping out of your comfort zone. Decisive action—grounded in preparation and calculated risk-taking—can lead to transformative results.

- **Career**:
    - Take on a challenging role that stretches your capabilities, such as leading a high-stakes project or switching industries. Bold moves often lead to significant growth.
    - For example, applying for a leadership position you feel slightly underqualified for might be the push you need to rise to the occasion.
- **Personal Life**:
    - Pursue passion projects or life goals despite uncertainties. Starting a creative endeavour, traveling solo, or learning a new skill may feel risky but can yield profound personal satisfaction.

4. Turning Points: Recognising and Seizing Opportunities

Scipio's Transition

The victories at Baecula and Ilipa marked a turning point in the Second Punic War. By shifting Rome's strategy from defense to offense, Scipio created the momentum that would ultimately lead to Hannibal's defeat at Zama.

- **Creating Momentum**:

Scipio didn't wait for opportunities to present themselves—he created them. Recognising the strategic significance of Spain, he seized control, laying the groundwork for Rome's dominance.

Modern Parallel

In life, recognising and acting on pivotal moments can redefine your trajectory. Often, the difference between success and stagnation lies in identifying these opportunities and acting decisively.

- **Professional**:
    - Spot emerging trends or gaps in the market and act before competitors. For example, developing

expertise in an underrepresented area of your field can set you apart.

    - Volunteer for leadership opportunities during organisational change—it's often in moments of uncertainty that new leaders emerge.

- **Personal**:
    - Realise when habits or relationships need to evolve. Taking proactive steps, like seeking counselling or adopting healthier routines, can turn challenges into turning points.

Practical Takeaways

Strategic Thinking Exercise

- Identify a long-term goal you want to achieve.
- List three potential obstacles that might hinder your progress.
- Develop strategies to address these obstacles, focusing on both immediate actions and future implications.

Adaptability Challenge

- Reflect on a recent setback or unexpected challenge in your life.
- What could you have done differently to adapt to the situation?
- Write down two alternative approaches you might use in the future when faced with similar challenges.

Bold Decision Test

- Think about an area in your life where hesitation is holding you back.
- Identify one bold, calculated step you can take this week to move forward.

- For example, it could be as simple as reaching out to a potential mentor or as significant as committing to a career change.

Turning Point Awareness

- Consider your current situation. Are there opportunities you haven't fully seized?
- What small step can you take today to turn those opportunities into defining moments?
- Reflect on how this action aligns with your long-term vision.

Closing Thought

Baecula and Ilipa weren't just battles—they were lessons in adaptability, foresight, and decisive action. Scipio's ability to plan for the long-term while seizing short-term opportunities offers a timeless framework for navigating life's challenges. Whether in your career, relationships, or personal goals, his principles remind us that success is a blend of preparation, flexibility, and boldness. Your turning points await—are you ready to seize them?

Chapter 4:

The Power of Adaptability – Handling Setbacks in Spain

Great leaders are not defined by how they perform in ideal circumstances but by how they respond when things go wrong. Scipio Africanus' campaign in Spain, while marked by triumphs, was also punctuated by setbacks—moments that tested his resolve and forced him to rethink his strategies. It was in these moments of adversity that Scipio's adaptability truly shone, solidifying his reputation as a commander who could turn the tide even in the face of disaster.

Setbacks in Spain: The Challenges of Command

When Scipio took command of Roman forces in Spain, he inherited more than an army; he inherited a theatre of war rife with complexities. The Carthaginians had been entrenched in the region for decades, forging alliances with local tribes and exploiting the challenging terrain to their advantage. Rome's presence, by contrast, was tenuous. Scipio faced enemies who knew the land intimately and wielded tactics tailored to its rugged hills, dense forests, and winding rivers. On top of that, he had to contend with Roman politics—divided loyalties among his officers and the Senate's scepticism of his youth and unconventional methods.

One of the most significant challenges came in the form of ambushes. The Carthaginians, aware of their disadvantage in open battle, frequently relied on guerrilla tactics, striking from hidden positions and retreating before the Romans could organise a counterattack. These ambushes disrupted supply lines, demoralised troops, and forced Scipio to reconsider how to fight an enemy that refused to meet him on traditional terms.

But Scipio's greatest strength was his refusal to let setbacks define him. Where others might have seen only obstacles, he saw opportunities to adapt, to learn, and to innovate. In doing so, he transformed each challenge into a stepping stone toward victory.

Adapting to the Terrain and Tactics

One of the key lessons Scipio learned in Spain was the importance of understanding the land. The terrain of the Iberian Peninsula was unlike the open plains of Italy, and traditional Roman tactics—linear formations, rigid discipline, and frontal assaults—often proved ineffective. Scipio realised that to succeed, he needed to fight like his enemies, embracing flexibility and taking advantage of the terrain.

To this end, he began training his troops in smaller, more mobile units, capable of responding quickly to unexpected attacks. He also made a point of studying the Carthaginian methods, learning from their successes and anticipating their moves. By doing so, he turned what had once been a weakness into a strength. Scipio's army became more agile, better able to navigate the rugged landscape, and more adept at countering ambushes.

But Scipio's adaptability wasn't limited to tactics. He also understood the importance of winning hearts and minds. Recognising that local tribes held the key to controlling the region, he worked to forge alliances with those who had grown disillusioned with Carthaginian rule. Through diplomacy, generosity, and a keen understanding of human nature, Scipio transformed potential adversaries into allies, further tipping the scales in Rome's favour.

The Ambush and the Counterattack: A Lesson in Resilience

One of the most striking examples of Scipio's adaptability came after a Carthaginian ambush caught his forces off guard. The enemy, hidden in the dense underbrush, launched a sudden and brutal attack on Scipio's column as it moved through a narrow pass. Chaos erupted as Roman soldiers struggled to defend themselves against an unseen foe, their formation breaking apart in the melee.

For many commanders, such an ambush would have spelled disaster. But Scipio, rather than retreating or succumbing to panic, rallied his men and devised a bold plan. Knowing the Carthaginians would not expect a counterattack in the darkness, he ordered his troops to regroup quietly and prepare for a nocturnal assault. As night fell, Scipio led a small, handpicked force through an unguarded path, flanking the enemy's position. At the signal, his soldiers descended on the unsuspecting Carthaginians, turning the ambush into a rout.

The surprise counterattack not only drove the Carthaginians into disarray but also restored his army's morale. It was a masterclass in resilience and resourcefulness, proving that even in the direst circumstances, a quick mind and decisive action could reverse the odds.

Lessons in Adaptability

Scipio's experiences in Spain hold valuable lessons for anyone facing setbacks in their own lives. His ability to adapt wasn't just a matter of survival; it was the key to his success. Here are some takeaways from his leadership during this period:

1. **Embrace Flexibility**:

Just as Scipio adjusted his tactics to suit the Iberian terrain, we too must be willing to change course when circumstances demand it. Rigidity in the face of new challenges often leads to failure, while flexibility opens the door to solutions.

2. **Learn from Your Adversaries**:

Scipio's willingness to study and adopt Carthaginian tactics highlights the importance of learning from those who oppose or challenge us. Whether it's a competitor in business or a difficult colleague, observing their methods can provide valuable insights.

3. **Turn Weakness into Strength**:

By training his army to be more agile and adaptable, Scipio transformed what had once been a liability into a competitive edge. In our own lives, we can achieve similar results by addressing our weaknesses head-on and finding ways to use them to our advantage.

4. **Think Creatively Under Pressure**:

Scipio's nocturnal counterattack is a testament to the power of creative problem-solving. When faced with a setback, ask yourself: What's the unexpected move that could turn the situation around?

5. **Leverage Relationships**:

Scipio's diplomacy with local tribes underscores the importance of building alliances. Whether in a professional or personal context, fostering strong relationships can help you navigate even the most challenging situations.

The Legacy of Adaptability

Scipio's setbacks in Spain were not failures; they were opportunities for growth. Each ambush, each political challenge, and each tactical dilemma forced him to think differently, to innovate, and to improve. By embracing adaptability, he not only overcame the immediate obstacles before him but also laid the foundation for his future victories.

For modern readers, Scipio's story is a reminder that setbacks are not the end of the road. Whether you're navigating a career challenge, dealing with unexpected changes, or facing personal difficulties, the ability to adapt is what will carry you through. Like Scipio, you have the power to turn adversity into opportunity, to learn from your experiences, and to emerge stronger on the other side.

Modern Parallel: Adapting to Setbacks

In life, setbacks are inevitable. Whether it's a missed promotion, a failed project, or a personal disappointment, everyone experiences moments where things don't go as planned. *What defines us isn't the failure itself but how we respond to it.* Do we dig in our heels and double down on approaches that aren't working, or do we pause, reassess, and adapt? Scipio Africanus' ability to thrive in adversity offers a timeless lesson: setbacks are not the end of the road—they're the start of a new path.

Adapting in the Professional World

Imagine a manager overseeing a struggling team. Deadlines are slipping, communication is breaking down, and morale is at an all-time low. The manager could stick rigidly to their original plan, insisting that the team simply work harder, or they could take a page from Scipio's playbook and adapt. By stepping back and analysing the situation—identifying weak points, consulting the team for input, and adjusting the strategy—they can turn things around. Adaptation isn't a sign of weakness; it's a hallmark of effective leadership.

The same principle applies to personal career setbacks. Perhaps you've been aiming for a promotion that hasn't materialised despite your best efforts. Doubling down—working longer hours, pushing harder—may not yield results if the underlying issue lies elsewhere. Instead, ask yourself: What's not working? Is there a skill I need to develop, a relationship I need to nurture, or a different approach I could try? By shifting your perspective, you open the door to new opportunities.

Adapting in Personal Life

Setbacks in personal life can be just as challenging. Consider someone trying to maintain a healthier lifestyle. Despite their best efforts—counting calories, exercising daily—the weight isn't coming off. It's tempting to push harder, restricting calories further or exercising to exhaustion. But this approach risks burnout and frustration. What if, instead, they adapted their strategy? Consulting a nutritionist, exploring new forms of exercise, or addressing underlying stressors could lead to a more sustainable and effective approach.

Adapting isn't about giving up on your goals—it's about finding better ways to achieve them. Scipio's experience in Spain, where he shifted tactics to outmanoeuvre the Carthaginians, is a powerful reminder that the willingness to change course can lead to greater success than stubbornly clinging to a failing plan.

Science Insight: Growth Mindset vs. Fixed Mindset

The concept of adapting to setbacks aligns closely with psychologist Carol Dweck's groundbreaking research on **growth mindset** and **fixed mindset**. These two mindsets determine how individuals view challenges and failures, shaping their ability to learn and grow.

1. **Fixed Mindset**:

Individuals with a fixed mindset believe that their abilities are static. They see failure as a reflection of their limitations, something to be avoided at all costs. For example:

- "I failed at this because I'm not smart enough."
- "If I don't succeed immediately, it means I'm not cut out for this."

This mindset often leads to defensiveness, blame-shifting, or avoidance, preventing growth and innovation.

2. **Growth Mindset**:

In contrast, a growth mindset views failure as an opportunity to learn. People with this mindset understand that abilities can be developed through effort, feedback, and persistence. They see setbacks as valuable feedback:

- "I didn't succeed this time, but I've learned what doesn't work."
- "What can I do differently next time?"

Scipio exemplified a growth mindset. When ambushed in Spain, he didn't see the setback as a personal failure or an insurmountable obstacle. Instead, he treated it as a learning opportunity, adapting his tactics and finding innovative solutions.

Practical Application: Building Your Growth Mindset

How can you develop a growth mindset and apply it to your own setbacks? It starts with reframing failure as feedback. Rather than seeing it as a dead end, view it as a stepping stone to success. Ask yourself:

- What went wrong, and why?
- What factors were within my control?
- What can I learn from this experience?

This shift in perspective not only reduces the fear of failure but also fosters resilience and creativity.

Reflective Journal Prompt

To help you integrate these lessons into your life, try this reflective journal exercise:

Step 1: Recall a Recent Failure

Think about a specific situation where you fell short of your goals. It could be a project that didn't meet expectations, a personal commitment you couldn't keep, or a relationship issue that didn't go as planned. Write down:

- The situation and the goal you were trying to achieve.
- What you did to try to succeed.
- The outcome and why it fell short of your expectations.

Step 2: Analyse the Causes

Reflect on what contributed to the failure. Be honest but compassionate with yourself:

- Were there external factors beyond your control? (*e.g., market conditions, timing, external pressures.*)
- Were there internal factors you could address? (*e.g., lack of preparation, poor communication, unrealistic expectations.*)

Step 3: Identify the Lessons

Ask yourself:

- What did this experience teach me about myself?
- What skills or strategies could I improve for next time?
- Did this failure reveal any opportunities I hadn't considered before?

Step 4: Create an Adaptation Plan

Use what you've learned to adjust your approach. For example:

- If a lack of planning contributed to your setback, commit to breaking future goals into smaller, actionable steps.
- If stress played a role, explore ways to prioritise self-care and manage your workload more effectively.
- If communication was an issue, consider seeking feedback or practising clearer ways to articulate your ideas.

Step 5: Look Forward

Write a short statement about how you plan to adapt moving forward. Focus on the positive changes you can make, rather than dwelling on the failure itself.

Closing Thought: Fail Forward

Setbacks are not failures—they are opportunities in disguise. Like Scipio adapting to the challenges of Spain, you have the power to learn, grow, and turn adversity into triumph. By embracing a growth mindset, you can transform even the most difficult experiences into stepping stones toward your goals. Remember, success isn't about avoiding failure; it's about how you respond to it. So take a deep breath, reflect, and adapt—your next breakthrough might be just around the corner.

Chapter 5:

Taking the Fight to Africa – Scipio's Bold Gamble

Every great leader has a moment when they must take a leap into the unknown, a gamble so bold that success seems improbable and failure catastrophic. For Scipio Africanus, that moment came with his decision to invade Africa, taking the fight directly to Carthage's homeland. This was not just a military strategy—it was a calculated risk that required immense personal conviction, political persuasion, and meticulous planning. Scipio's campaign in Africa became the turning point in the Second Punic War, a demonstration of his ability to not only envision success but to lay the groundwork for achieving it.

A Bold Proposal: Convincing Rome

By the time Scipio proposed his African campaign, Rome had endured years of attrition warfare against Hannibal in Italy. Hannibal's presence, while less devastating than in his early campaigns, remained a persistent threat, draining resources and morale. Many in the Roman Senate believed the safest course of action was to continue defensive operations, avoiding unnecessary risks. Scipio, however, saw a different path.

Rather than fight Hannibal on Roman soil indefinitely, Scipio proposed an audacious plan: to invade Carthage's homeland and force Hannibal to abandon Italy to defend his city. It was a daring move that many senators viewed as reckless. The risks were undeniable. If Scipio failed, he would not only lose Rome's army in Africa but also leave the Republic vulnerable to renewed Carthaginian aggression.

To convince the Senate, Scipio relied on his characteristic blend of logic and charisma. He argued that Rome could not afford to fight a defensive war forever—that true victory required boldness. Scipio's previous successes in Spain, particularly his capture of New Carthage, lent credibility to his vision. His confidence was infectious; he painted a picture of triumph so vivid that even the most cautious senators were swayed. Ultimately, he secured the Senate's approval, though they provided only limited support, placing much of the responsibility squarely on his shoulders.

Meticulous Planning: Preparing for the Gamble

Scipio knew that success in Africa would depend on more than just bravery. Every detail of the campaign had to be meticulously planned. Unlike in Spain, where he could rely on Roman supply lines, Africa would present logistical challenges that required foresight and adaptability.

- **Assembling the Army**:

Scipio recruited a diverse force, including veterans from his campaigns in Spain and new recruits eager to prove themselves. He also trained his men rigorously, preparing them for the unfamiliar terrain and conditions they would face in Africa.

- **Studying the Terrain**:

Scipio immersed himself in understanding the geography of North Africa, identifying potential landing sites, supply routes, and strategic strongholds. He also studied Carthaginian tactics, anticipating how they might defend their homeland.

- **Anticipating Hannibal**:

Scipio knew that his ultimate goal—drawing Hannibal out of Italy—would require not only military success but also psychological warfare. By threatening Carthage itself, he aimed to force Hannibal into a defensive posture, disrupting his momentum and placing him at a disadvantage.

The Masinissa Alliance: A Diplomatic Triumph

One of the most critical elements of Scipio's plan was his alliance with Masinissa, the Numidian king. Numidia, located in present-day Algeria and Tunisia, was home to some of the finest cavalry in the ancient world. These mounted warriors, known for their speed and agility, had long been a key component of

Carthaginian armies. By securing Masinissa's support, Scipio not only weakened Carthage but also gained a powerful asset for his own campaign.

Scipio's meeting with Masinissa was as much about diplomacy as it was about strategy. The young Roman commander approached the Numidian king not as a conqueror but as a partner, appealing to their shared interest in weakening Carthage. Masinissa, who had his own grievances against Carthage, saw in Scipio a kindred spirit—a leader willing to take bold action for a greater cause.

The alliance proved invaluable. Numidian cavalry played a decisive role in the African campaign, providing Scipio with a mobile and versatile force that could outmanoeuvre Carthaginian units. Beyond their tactical value, the Numidians symbolised Scipio's ability to forge connections and build coalitions, a skill that would define his career.

The Risks of Boldness

While Scipio's decision to invade Africa was visionary, it was not without its critics. Many in Rome feared that he was overextending, gambling the Republic's future on an untested strategy. Even among his own officers, there were doubts about the feasibility of the campaign. Yet Scipio remained undeterred. He understood that all great victories require an element of risk and that playing it safe would only prolong the war.

Scipio's gamble also extended to his leadership style. By placing himself at the forefront of such a high-stakes mission, he risked not only his career but also his reputation. Failure in Africa would have been catastrophic, not just for Rome but for Scipio personally. Yet it was precisely this willingness to embrace risk that inspired his troops. They saw in him a leader who believed in their mission with unwavering conviction, and they were willing to follow him into the unknown.

Lessons in Strategy and Resilience

Scipio's decision to take the fight to Africa offers enduring lessons for anyone facing high-stakes challenges. His ability to balance boldness with meticulous planning, to forge alliances in the face of adversity, and to inspire confidence in those around him is a blueprint for success in both leadership and life.

1. **Boldness Requires Preparation**:

Taking risks doesn't mean acting recklessly. Scipio's invasion of Africa was daring, but it was also underpinned by careful planning and thorough preparation.

2. **Leverage Alliances**:

Success often depends on the strength of your relationships. Just as Scipio secured Masinissa's support, we too can achieve greater outcomes by building and nurturing partnerships.

3. **Vision Inspires Confidence**:

Scipio's ability to articulate a clear vision of victory convinced even sceptics to support his plan. In our own lives, having a strong sense of purpose and direction can inspire others to believe in us and our goals.

4. **Embrace Calculated Risks**:

Playing it safe rarely leads to transformative success. By embracing risk while mitigating potential downsides, Scipio achieved a breakthrough that changed the course of history.

The Path to Zama

Scipio's gamble in Africa set the stage for one of the most famous battles in history: the Battle of Zama. But the seeds of that victory were sown long before the first spear was thrown. They were planted in Scipio's bold decision to take the fight to Carthage, in his meticulous planning, and in his ability to forge alliances with leaders like Masinissa.

As we reflect on this chapter of Scipio's life, it's worth asking: What bold moves are you willing to make to achieve your goals? How can you prepare for the risks ahead? And who might become your "Masinissa," supporting you on your journey?

Scipio's story reminds us that great victories are not won by chance—they are the result of vision, preparation, and the courage to take risks. The path may be uncertain, but the rewards can be transformative.

Modern Parallel: Taking Bold Risks to Disrupt Stagnation

Life often has a way of lulling us into comfort zones—predictable routines, safe decisions, and paths of least resistance. But just as Scipio Africanus recognised that playing defence against Hannibal would only prolong Rome's struggles, we too must confront the reality that real progress often requires bold, calculated risks. Whether it's making a career change, pursuing a creative passion, or challenging the status quo in your personal life, bold risks can be the catalyst that shakes us out of stagnation and sets us on the path to growth.

Breaking Free from Stagnation

Imagine you've been in the same job for years. While it pays the bills and offers a sense of stability, it leaves you feeling uninspired and unfulfilled. You dream of starting your own business, writing a book, or pursuing a career that aligns more closely with your passions. Yet, fear holds you back—the fear of financial instability, of failure, or of stepping into the unknown.

This is where Scipio's example becomes instructive. When he proposed taking the fight to Africa, the Roman Senate balked at the idea. It was safer, they argued, to continue fighting Hannibal on Italian soil, even if it meant a drawn-out war. But Scipio understood that safety and stagnation often go hand in hand. By daring to disrupt the status quo, he created the conditions for a decisive victory.

Similarly, disrupting stagnation in our own lives requires the courage to take risks. This doesn't mean acting recklessly—it means embracing change with careful planning and a clear vision of the rewards. The process can be daunting, but the potential for growth, fulfilment, and transformation often outweighs the risks.

The Psychology of Risk-Taking

Why do bold risks feel so intimidating? The answer lies in our brain's natural inclination to avoid uncertainty. Humans are hardwired to favour predictability and stability, as these conditions historically ensured survival. But in the modern world, this aversion to risk can become a barrier to personal and professional growth.

Psychologists have identified several key factors that influence our ability to take risks:

1. **Fear of Failure**:

Failure is often perceived as a personal flaw rather than a learning opportunity. This mindset can paralyse decision-making, keeping us tethered to the familiar.

2. **Loss Aversion**:

Studies show that people fear losing something they already have more than they value gaining something new. This bias makes it difficult to leave behind the known, even for a potentially better future.

3. **Overestimating Risks**:

The human brain tends to exaggerate the potential downsides of a decision while underestimating its rewards. This skewed perception can make risks appear more daunting than they actually are.

4. **Underestimating Resilience**:

People often forget how capable they are of bouncing back from setbacks. This underestimation of resilience amplifies the fear of taking risks.

However, there's good news: with the right preparation and perspective, you can overcome these barriers. The key lies in reframing risk as an opportunity rather than a threat.

Overcoming Fear Through Preparation

Scipio's decision to invade Africa wasn't made on a whim. He understood the stakes and prepared meticulously, ensuring that the risks were calculated rather than reckless. This same principle applies to modern decision-making. By investing time in preparation, you can reduce uncertainty and increase your confidence in the path ahead.

Consider the example of someone contemplating a career change. Instead of quitting their job impulsively, they could take the following steps:

- **Research the New Path**: Gather information about the industry, required skills, and potential challenges.
- **Build a Safety Net**: Save money or secure a part-time role to provide financial stability during the transition.
- **Test the Waters**: Take on freelance work, internships, or side projects to gain experience and validate your interest.
- **Seek Guidance**: Consult mentors or professionals in the field for advice and insights.

Preparation not only mitigates risk but also helps you approach bold decisions with a clear head, allowing you to focus on the potential rewards rather than the fear of failure.

Reframing Perspective

Sometimes, the greatest risk is not taking one at all. Staying in a stagnant situation—whether in your career, relationships, or personal development—can lead to regret, dissatisfaction, and missed opportunities. Reframing your perspective can make risks feel less intimidating and more empowering. Ask yourself:

- What's the worst-case scenario? Can I recover from it?
- What's the best-case scenario? How would it improve my life?
- What's the cost of doing nothing? How will I feel if I let this opportunity pass me by?

By shifting your focus to the potential rewards and your ability to handle setbacks, you can approach risks with greater clarity and confidence.

Workbook: Evaluating Risks vs. Rewards

Use this decision-making tool to evaluate a major life choice and determine whether it's worth pursuing.

Step 1: Define the Goal

What bold step are you considering? Be specific. For example:

- "I want to start my own business."
- "I want to move to a new city."
- "I want to leave my current job to pursue a creative career."

Step 2: Identify Potential Risks

List the possible downsides of this decision. Be honest but avoid catastrophising. For example:

- Financial instability during the transition.
- Difficulty adjusting to a new environment or role.
- Potential for initial failure or rejection.

Step 3: Identify Potential Rewards

List the possible benefits. Be as detailed as possible. For example:

- Greater fulfilment and alignment with your passions.
- Improved quality of life or personal growth.
- Opportunities for long-term success and happiness.

Step 4: Assess Your Resilience

How well-equipped are you to handle the risks? Consider your:

- Support network (family, friends, mentors).
- Skills and resources (savings, experience, adaptability).
- Past experiences of overcoming challenges.

Step 5: Develop a Risk Mitigation Plan

What steps can you take to reduce the risks? For example:

- Build a financial cushion to cover expenses.
- Upskill or gain experience in your desired field.
- Create a contingency plan in case things don't go as expected.

Step 6: Make Your Decision

Weigh the risks against the rewards. If the potential benefits outweigh the downsides—and if you have a plan to manage the risks—consider taking the leap.

Step 7: Commit to Action

If you decide to move forward, outline the first steps you'll take to turn your goal into reality. Set a timeline and hold yourself accountable.

Closing Thought: Bold Risks, Big Rewards

Taking bold risks isn't easy—it requires courage, preparation, and a willingness to step into the unknown. But as Scipio Africanus demonstrated, it's often the boldest moves that yield the greatest rewards. Whether you're aiming to disrupt stagnation in your career, relationships, or personal growth, remember: progress comes to those who dare to act. Prepare thoroughly, trust your resilience, and take the leap. The rewards may be greater than you ever imagined.

Chapter 6:

Building Alliances – The Value of Teamwork

No leader achieves greatness alone. Even the most brilliant strategist or visionary relies on the strength of those around them. For Scipio Africanus, this truth was never more apparent than during his African campaign. Recognising the limitations of his resources and the challenges of fighting on foreign soil, Scipio turned to one of the most powerful tools in his arsenal: diplomacy. By forging alliances with African leaders like Masinissa, he transformed potential obstacles into opportunities, creating a network of support that would prove decisive in the climactic Battle of Zama.

The Art of Diplomacy: Building Bridges

When Scipio landed in Africa, he understood that military might alone wouldn't be enough to secure victory. Carthage was deeply entrenched in the region, with local allies and a thorough knowledge of the terrain. To level the playing field, Scipio sought to win over local leaders who had grown disillusioned with Carthaginian rule. His approach was as strategic as any battlefield manoeuvre: he didn't demand loyalty or use threats; instead, he appealed to shared interests and offered mutually beneficial partnerships.

One of Scipio's key strengths was his ability to understand the motivations of others. He recognised that loyalty often stemmed from practical concerns rather than sentiment. By promising protection, resources, and respect, he positioned himself as a more attractive ally than Carthage. Scipio's genuine respect for his allies further cemented these relationships. Unlike many Roman commanders, who saw non-Romans as inferior, Scipio treated his partners as equals, earning their trust and cooperation.

Masinissa: The Kingmaker

Of all Scipio's alliances, his partnership with Masinissa, the king of Numidia, was the most critical. Masinissa was a brilliant leader and an exceptional cavalry commander, whose forces were renowned for their speed and agility. Initially aligned with Carthage, Masinissa had grown frustrated with his treatment by Carthaginian leaders and was eager for a new ally who respected his ambitions.

Scipio approached Masinissa not as a conqueror but as a collaborator. He recognised the Numidian king's potential and promised to support his bid for greater power in exchange for loyalty. This offer appealed to Masinissa's desire for independence and prestige, and he agreed to join forces with Scipio.

Masinissa's cavalry became a game-changing asset for the Roman army. In the Battle of Zama, his forces played a pivotal role in neutralising Hannibal's legendary cavalry, shifting the balance of power in favour of Rome. The alliance wasn't just a tactical success—it was a testament to Scipio's ability to identify and cultivate partnerships that amplified his strengths.

The Power of Teamwork

Scipio's success in Africa was a direct result of his ability to build and lead a cohesive team. He understood that leadership wasn't about dictating orders but about aligning the goals and talents of diverse individuals toward a common purpose. This principle is as relevant today as it was on the battlefields of antiquity. Whether you're managing a workplace team, organising a community project, or navigating family dynamics, the ability to foster collaboration and build trust is key to achieving success.

Scipio's alliance with Masinissa also highlights the importance of recognising and leveraging complementary strengths. Scipio knew that his Roman infantry alone couldn't match the versatility of Hannibal's forces. By partnering with Masinissa, he gained a cavalry force that could outmanoeuvre and outpace the enemy, filling a critical gap in his own army. This willingness to rely on others' expertise is a hallmark of effective leadership.

Lessons in Diplomacy and Teamwork

Scipio's alliances in Africa offer timeless lessons for building strong, effective teams:

1. **Understand What Others Value**:

Scipio's ability to persuade Masinissa stemmed from his understanding of the Numidian king's ambitions. Similarly, when building partnerships in your own life, take the time to understand what motivates others and how you can align your goals with theirs.

2. **Offer Mutual Benefits**:

Partnerships thrive when both parties see value in the relationship. Scipio didn't demand loyalty without offering something in return; he created alliances based on shared interests. In any team setting, think about how you can create win-win scenarios that benefit everyone involved.

3. **Respect and Empower Your Allies**:

Scipio's respect for Masinissa and his other allies set him apart from many Roman leaders. By treating his partners as equals and recognising their contributions, he built trust and loyalty. In your own interactions, focus on empowering others rather than seeking to dominate or control.

4. **Leverage Diverse Strengths**:

Scipio's partnership with Masinissa wasn't about duplicating his own abilities; it was about complementing them. In team settings, look for individuals who bring unique skills and perspectives to the table, creating a more well-rounded and effective group.

5. **Communicate a Clear Vision**:

Scipio's alliances succeeded because he articulated a compelling vision of victory. People are more likely to follow you when they understand and believe in the goal. As a leader, ensure that your vision is clear, inspiring, and inclusive.

The Role of Trust

At the heart of Scipio's alliances was trust. This trust wasn't blind; it was earned through consistent actions and mutual respect. Scipio didn't see his allies as tools to be used and discarded; he saw them as partners in a shared endeavour. This trust was reciprocated, creating a network of relationships that extended beyond the battlefield.

In modern terms, trust is the foundation of any successful team or partnership. Without it, even the most talented group of individuals will struggle to achieve their goals. Building trust requires honesty, transparency, and a willingness to listen and adapt. It also means recognising and valuing the contributions of others, as Scipio did with Masinissa.

Closing Thought: The Value of Alliances

Scipio Africanus' ability to build alliances wasn't just a tactical skill—it was a reflection of his understanding of human nature. He knew that true strength comes not from standing alone but from working together. His partnership with Masinissa was more than a military alliance; it was a model of collaboration and mutual respect that changed the course of history.

As you reflect on your own life, consider the alliances you've built—or those you have yet to form. Who are the "Masinissas" in your life, the people whose strengths complement your own? How can you build stronger, more trusting relationships with those around you? And how can you, like Scipio, inspire loyalty and collaboration by treating others with respect and empowering them to succeed?

Scipio's victory at Zama was a triumph of teamwork as much as strategy, a reminder that even the boldest vision is best achieved with the support of others. Whether in the workplace, the community, or your personal life, the lessons of Scipio's alliances can help you build the connections that lead to lasting success.

Modern Parallel: Building Strong Networks for Success

In both ancient battlefields and modern boardrooms, the value of strong relationships cannot be overstated. Scipio Africanus' success in Africa didn't rest solely on military might or tactical brilliance—it was deeply rooted in his ability to form alliances and build trust. In today's world, this translates to the importance of building and maintaining personal and professional networks. These connections provide support, open doors to new opportunities, and help us navigate the challenges of life and work with greater ease.

Just as Scipio forged a pivotal alliance with Masinissa by understanding his motivations and showing respect, we too can create meaningful connections by applying emotional intelligence and a strategic approach to our relationships.

The Power of Networks

Imagine you're trying to advance in your career, launch a business, or even navigate a personal challenge. The strength of your network often determines your ability to succeed. Consider these examples:

- **In the workplace**: Professionals with strong networks are more likely to hear about job opportunities, gain mentors, or access resources that help them excel.
- **In personal life**: A supportive circle of friends and family provides emotional resilience, guidance, and a sense of belonging.
- **In entrepreneurship**: Successful entrepreneurs often cite their networks as the key to finding investors, partners, and customers.

Building a network isn't just about knowing the right people—it's about creating genuine, reciprocal relationships that stand the test of time. The foundation of such relationships lies in emotional intelligence.

Emotional Intelligence: The Key to Connection

Emotional intelligence (EQ) is the ability to understand, manage, and express your emotions while recognising and influencing the emotions of others. It's the secret sauce behind building trust, resolving conflicts, and fostering collaboration. Here's how EQ plays a role in strengthening networks:

1. **Empathy**:

Understanding what others value or need is critical to forming meaningful relationships. Scipio's alliance with Masinissa worked because he recognised and addressed Masinissa's aspirations. In your own life, showing empathy—whether by listening actively or offering support—can deepen connections.

2. **Self-awareness**:

Knowing your strengths, weaknesses, and communication style helps you present yourself authentically. People are drawn to those who are genuine and comfortable in their own skin.

3. **Social skills**:

Strong relationships require effective communication, from active listening to non verbal cues. Scipio's diplomatic finesse wasn't about grand speeches—it was about understanding his audience and tailoring his approach.

4. **Adaptability**:

Just as Scipio adapted his strategies to suit different allies, building strong networks requires flexibility. Not all relationships are the same, and adjusting your approach based on context is key.

5. **Building trust**:

Trust is earned through consistent actions, honesty, and reliability. Scipio didn't demand loyalty—he earned it by treating his allies with respect and delivering on his promises.

Creating Your "Relationship Map"

A practical way to strengthen your network is by visualising it as a map. This exercise will help you identify the relationships you rely on, the ones that need nurturing, and the areas where you can build new connections.

Step 1: Draw Your Network

Take a blank sheet of paper or open a digital tool and create a map of your current relationships. Start with:

- **Close Connections**: Family, close friends, mentors, or trusted colleagues.
- **Professional Contacts**: Current or former colleagues, clients, business partners.
- **Community and Social Circles**: Neighbours, club members, or acquaintances from hobbies or volunteer work.

Place yourself at the centre and draw lines connecting you to each person or group.

Step 2: Categorise Relationships

Label each connection based on its nature:

- **Strong**: Relationships that are close, supportive, and mutually beneficial.
- **Moderate**: Relationships that are friendly but could benefit from more interaction or deeper trust.
- **Weak**: Acquaintances or people you've lost touch with but would like to reconnect with.

Step 3: Identify Gaps

Look for areas where your network might need strengthening:

- Are there weak relationships you'd like to rebuild?
- Are there missing types of connections? (e.g., mentors in a specific field, peers who share similar goals.)

- Do you lack diversity in your network? (e.g., connections from different industries, backgrounds, or perspectives.)

Step 4: Set Goals

Choose three relationships to focus on over the next month:

1. **Strengthen a Moderate Connection**: For example, reconnect with a colleague over coffee or reach out to a distant friend.
2. **Deepen a Strong Connection**: Spend quality time with a close friend or mentor to strengthen your bond.
3. **Build a New Connection**: Attend a networking event, join a club, or reach out to someone you admire on social media.

Taking Action: Strengthening Your Network

Once you've mapped your relationships and set goals, it's time to take action. Here are some strategies inspired by Scipio's diplomacy:

1. **Be Proactive**:

Don't wait for opportunities to arise—create them. Send a thoughtful message, schedule a meeting, or offer support without being asked.

2. **Add Value**:

Relationships thrive on reciprocity. Look for ways to help others, whether by sharing knowledge, offering introductions, or simply being a good listener.

3. **Stay Consistent**:

Building trust takes time. Show up consistently for the people in your network, even if it's through small gestures like checking in regularly.

4. **Leverage Shared Interests**:

Common goals or values strengthen bonds. Whether it's a shared professional objective or a mutual hobby, use these connections to deepen relationships.

5. **Be Genuine**:

Authenticity is key. Scipio's success wasn't based on manipulation—it was grounded in mutual respect and honest intentions. Be sincere in your interactions, and people will respond in kind.

The Bigger Picture

Your network is more than a collection of contacts—it's a living, evolving ecosystem that supports your growth, resilience, and success. By investing time and effort into building strong connections, you're not only enriching your own life but also creating opportunities to make a positive impact on others.

Like Scipio Africanus, you have the ability to forge alliances that go beyond mere transactions. These are relationships built on trust, mutual benefit, and a shared vision of success. Whether you're rallying a team at work, leaning on a friend for support, or seeking advice from a mentor, the strength of your network can carry you through life's challenges and opportunities.

Closing Thought: The Value of Connection

Scipio's alliance with Masinissa wasn't just a tactical manoeuvre—it was a masterclass in the power of connection. It reminds us that true strength lies not in standing alone but in standing together. As you create your relationship map and take steps to strengthen your network, remember: every meaningful connection you build is an investment in your future. Reach out, nurture relationships, and watch your network—and your life—flourish.

Chapter 7:

The Road to Zama – Preparation and Confidence

Every great story builds to a climactic moment when preparation meets destiny. For Scipio Africanus, that moment was the Battle of Zama. Facing Hannibal, one of history's most legendary generals, on African soil, Scipio knew the stakes couldn't be higher. This wasn't just a battle for victory—it was a battle for the future of Rome. His calm demeanour and meticulous preparation in the lead-up to Zama not only gave his troops the confidence to face a formidable foe but also demonstrated the power of readiness in overcoming even the most daunting challenges.

Preparing for Hannibal's Elephants

The elephants. These massive beasts were the terror of ancient battlefields, used by Hannibal to devastating effect in previous campaigns. With their sheer size and ability to scatter infantry, war elephants were often the trump card that gave Carthaginian armies an edge. Scipio understood that if he failed to counter this threat, Zama could be lost before it even began. His preparation for this challenge was nothing short of extraordinary.

Scipio studied reports of Hannibal's previous battles, particularly his use of elephants at Trebia and Cannae. He analysed their weaknesses—how they panicked when disoriented, how they struggled in tight formations, and how they could turn on their own forces if their handlers lost control. Armed with this knowledge, Scipio devised a plan that would neutralise the Carthaginian advantage.

Instead of the traditional tightly packed Roman lines, Scipio arranged his troops in staggered columns with wide lanes running between them. These lanes were designed as elephant corridors—paths the elephants could charge down without causing significant harm to the Roman ranks. Infantry armed with javelins and flaming torches stood ready at the edges of the lanes to harass and disorient the elephants, driving them into chaos. Behind the infantry, cavalry units prepared to exploit any openings created by the confusion.

This strategic brilliance wasn't just about countering the elephants; it was about turning Hannibal's greatest asset into a liability. By planning for the worst-case scenario, Scipio transformed a potential disaster into an opportunity.

Training for Confidence

Preparation wasn't limited to strategy. Scipio understood that his troops' confidence would be just as critical as their formation. Many of his soldiers had never faced elephants in battle, and fear of the unknown could easily undermine their resolve. To combat this, Scipio introduced rigorous training exercises designed to familiarise his men with the sight, sound, and chaos of charging elephants.

- **Mock Charges**: Scipio arranged for mock elephant charges using large, mobile structures pulled by oxen to simulate the beasts. Soldiers practised holding their positions and manoeuvring into the staggered formations that would protect them in the actual battle.
- **Noise Conditioning**: Elephants were as terrifying to the ears as they were to the eyes. Scipio ensured his troops were exposed to loud, sudden noises during training to desensitise them to the cacophony of battle.
- **Team Cohesion**: Scipio emphasised the importance of discipline and trust within the ranks. He knew that fear could cause disorder, but unity would keep his lines intact. Through repeated drills and clear communication, he instilled a sense of camaraderie and mutual reliance among his men.

These exercises weren't just about preparing for battle—they were about fostering belief. Scipio's soldiers entered the field at Zama not as individuals, but as a cohesive unit, each member confident in their role and their commander's plan.

Calm in the Face of Chaos

One of the most remarkable aspects of Scipio's leadership was his unshakable calm. In the days leading up to Zama, when anxiety among the troops was at its peak, Scipio exuded confidence. He spoke to his men not as a distant commander but as one of them, acknowledging their fears while emphasising their strength. He reminded them of their victories in Spain and Africa, urging them to see Zama not as a moment of dread but as an opportunity to bring an end to years of hardship.

A particularly famous anecdote from this period illustrates Scipio's composure. On the eve of the battle, he reportedly walked among his troops, sharing stories, cracking jokes, and reassuring them with his steady presence. His demeanour was infectious—if Scipio could face Hannibal without fear, so could they. His ability to project confidence under pressure became a rallying point for his soldiers, turning apprehension into anticipation.

Lessons from Scipio's Preparation

Scipio's road to Zama offers timeless lessons in the power of preparation and confidence. Whether you're facing a career-defining presentation, a personal challenge, or a high-stakes decision, his approach provides a blueprint for success:

1. **Anticipate Challenges**:

Just as Scipio planned for Hannibal's elephants, take the time to identify potential obstacles in your own path. Ask yourself: What's the worst-case scenario, and how can I prepare for it?

2. **Train for Success**:

Preparation isn't just about knowing your strategy—it's about practising it. Repetition builds confidence, whether it's rehearsing a speech, mastering a new skill, or strengthening a team dynamic.

3. **Foster Unity**:

Success often depends on the people around you. Invest in building trust, communication, and collaboration within your team or support network.

4. **Project Confidence**:

Even if you're nervous, your attitude can influence those around you. Approach challenges with calm determination, and others will follow your lead.

5. **Turn Weakness into Strength**:

Like Scipio's use of the elephant corridors, look for ways to turn potential disadvantages into opportunities. This mindset shifts your focus from fear to innovation.

The Calm Before the Storm

As Scipio's army marched to meet Hannibal's forces on the plains of Zama, the stakes couldn't have been higher. Rome's future rested on the outcome of this battle, yet Scipio's troops carried with them a sense of purpose and belief. They had seen their commander's confidence, trained for the challenges ahead, and trusted in the strategy that had been meticulously crafted for this moment.

Scipio's leadership on the road to Zama reminds us that preparation isn't just about logistics—it's about mindset. By anticipating obstacles, practising resilience, and inspiring confidence in ourselves and others, we can face even the most daunting challenges with strength and clarity.

As the armies lined up for battle and the war elephants began their charge, Scipio's soldiers stood firm, ready to meet their ultimate test. They had been prepared for this moment—not just physically, but mentally. In the chapters ahead, we'll see how Scipio's strategy and leadership unfolded on the battlefield, culminating in one of the most decisive victories in history. For now, let his preparation and poise serve as a reminder that success is built long before the battle begins.

Modern Parallel: Preparing for High-Stakes Moments

Life is filled with high-stakes moments that demand our best—exams, job interviews, major presentations, or critical negotiations. These events can feel overwhelming, much like the pressure Scipio Africanus must have faced as he prepared for the Battle of Zama. Yet, just as Scipio's meticulous preparation transformed anxiety into readiness, we too can approach our challenges with confidence and composure if we prepare effectively.

Preparation is not just about knowing the material or having a plan; it's about mental readiness. Fear of failure and performance anxiety are common obstacles, but they can be mitigated through deliberate strategies. By adopting techniques like visualisation and creating a structured "battle plan," we can face our most daunting challenges with Scipio-like resolve.

Preparation for Exams, Presentations, and Negotiations

Exams: Turning Knowledge into Confidence

For students, exams often feel like the intellectual equivalent of a battlefield. Success depends on more than just studying—it requires the ability to recall and apply knowledge under pressure. Here's how preparation can make all the difference:

- **Understand the Terrain**: Just as Scipio studied Hannibal's tactics, understand the exam format, key topics, and likely challenges. Review past papers or practice questions to gain familiarity.

- **Build Stamina**: Scipio's troops trained for the chaos of battle; you can train your brain for the mental endurance exams require. Timed mock tests replicate the conditions and help you manage your time effectively.

- **Calm the Mind**: Anxiety can cloud your thinking. Incorporate relaxation techniques like deep breathing or short meditative breaks into your study routine.

Presentations: Commanding the Room

Delivering a presentation can feel as intimidating as leading troops into battle. The stakes—your reputation, a potential promotion, or a new client—add to the pressure. Preparation here is key:

- **Craft Your Message**: Like Scipio's carefully planned strategies, your presentation should have a clear structure. Know your audience, anticipate questions, and build your narrative around a core message.
- **Rehearse, Then Rehearse Again**: Practise until your delivery feels natural. Record yourself to identify areas for improvement, and test your presentation on a trusted friend or colleague.
- **Visualise Success**: Imagine yourself delivering the presentation with confidence, engaging your audience and achieving your desired outcome. This mental rehearsal reduces anxiety and primes your mind for success.

Negotiations: Strategising for Victory

Negotiations, whether for a salary increase or a business deal, require a balance of preparation and adaptability:

- **Know Your Goals**: Like Scipio's strategic objectives, define what you want to achieve and identify your non-negotiables.
- **Understand the Opposition**: Research the other party's interests, priorities, and potential constraints. This insight gives you an edge.
- **Plan for the Unexpected**: Anticipate counterarguments or objections and prepare flexible responses, just as Scipio adjusted his tactics during battle.

Science Insight: The Power of Visualisation

One of the most effective tools for preparation is visualisation—a technique used by athletes, performers, and even military leaders to build confidence and reduce anxiety. Visualisation works by creating a mental blueprint of success, helping you mentally rehearse a situation before it occurs.

How It Works

The brain doesn't distinguish strongly between real and imagined experiences. When you vividly visualise yourself succeeding, your brain activates the same neural pathways as if you were actually performing the task. This primes your mind and body to replicate those successful actions in real life.

Benefits of Visualisation

1. **Reduces Anxiety**: Imagining yourself handling challenges with composure lowers stress and increases your sense of control.

2. **Builds Confidence**: Repeatedly visualising success helps you internalise the belief that you are capable of achieving your goals.

3. **Improves Focus**: Visualisation helps clarify your objectives and the steps required to achieve them.

How to Use Visualisation

1. Find a quiet spacc whcrc you won't be interrupted.

2. Close your eyes and imagine the scenario in vivid detail. If it's a presentation, picture the room, the audience, and yourself speaking confidently.

3. Focus on positive outcomes. See yourself overcoming obstacles, answering questions effectively, or negotiating with ease.

4. Repeat this process regularly in the days leading up to the event.

Workbook: Creating Your Battle Plan

To help you prepare for your next major challenge, use this step-by-step workbook to create a personalised "battle plan."

Step 1: Define Your Objective

Clearly state what you want to achieve. Be specific and measurable. For example:

- "I want to score 85% on my exam."
- "I want to deliver a presentation that secures client approval."
- "I want to negotiate a 10% salary increase."

Step 2: Assess the Terrain

Identify the key elements of the situation:

- **Challenges**: What obstacles might you face? (e.g., tricky exam questions, tough audience questions, negotiation resistance.)
- **Resources**: What tools or support can you use? (e.g., textbooks, mentors, presentation aids.)
- **Stakeholders**: Who is involved, and what are their priorities? (e.g., examiners, clients, your boss.)

Step 3: Break It Down

Divide your preparation into manageable steps:

1. Research or study the key topics.
2. Practise essential skills (e.g., mock tests, presentation rehearsals).
3. Prepare for potential challenges (e.g., answering tough questions, handling objections).

Set deadlines for each step to ensure steady progress.

Step 4: Visualise Success

Dedicate 5–10 minutes daily to visualising yourself achieving your goal. Imagine yourself:

- Answering questions confidently during the exam.
- Delivering your presentation with poise.
- Negotiating assertively and securing the deal.

Step 5: Test Your Readiness

Simulate the event to identify areas for improvement:

- Take a timed practice exam.
- Deliver your presentation to a small audience and gather feedback.
- Role-play the negotiation with a friend or mentor.

Step 6: Prepare for Contingencies

Identify potential "what-ifs" and plan your responses:

- What if you forget a key point during the presentation? (Prepare notes or prompts.)
- What if the negotiation stalls? (Have alternatives ready.)
- What if anxiety strikes? (Use relaxation techniques like deep breathing.)

Step 7: Execute with Confidence

On the day of the event, trust your preparation. Remember:

- You've anticipated challenges and prepared for them.
- You've practised and visualised success.
- You're ready to adapt if necessary.

Closing Thought: Preparation is Power

Scipio Africanus' triumph at Zama wasn't just the result of courage—it was the culmination of meticulous preparation. His ability to anticipate challenges, train his troops, and inspire confidence allowed him to face one of history's greatest generals with unwavering resolve. Whether you're facing an exam, a presentation, or a negotiation, the same principles apply. By preparing thoroughly, visualising success, and creating a structured plan, you can turn anxiety into readiness and achieve your goals with Scipio-like determination. The battlefield may look different, but the path to victory remains the same.

Chapter 8:

The Battle of Zama – Turning Adversity into Triumph

The Battle of Zama was more than a clash of armies; it was the culmination of years of conflict, strategy, and personal growth. On one side stood Hannibal Barca, a name synonymous with military genius, whose campaigns had brought Rome to its knees. On the other was Scipio Africanus, a young commander who had risen through adversity to become Rome's greatest hope. The stakes couldn't have been higher: Rome's survival and Carthage's future hung in the balance. Yet, in this epic showdown, it wasn't brute force that determined the outcome—it was Scipio's ability to outthink, outmanoeuvre, and adapt to an ever-changing battlefield.

Outmanoeuvring Hannibal

Hannibal entered the Battle of Zama as a legend. He had spent over a decade in Italy, defeating Roman armies with innovative tactics and near-supernatural cunning. His war elephants, cavalry, and seasoned infantry made him a formidable opponent, even on the defensive. Scipio knew this battle would require not only his troops' courage but also his own strategic brilliance.

Understanding Hannibal's Strengths

Scipio's first advantage was his deep understanding of Hannibal's tactics. He had studied the Carthaginian general's victories, particularly his use of ambushes, cavalry, and psychological warfare. Hannibal's greatest strength was his ability to exploit weaknesses in rigid Roman formations. Scipio's solution? Adaptability.

Instead of relying on traditional Roman tactics, Scipio tailored his approach to counter Hannibal's every move. He understood that Hannibal's war elephants, while terrifying, could be neutralised through careful preparation. His staggered infantry lines, first tested in training, would allow the elephants to pass harmlessly through Roman ranks while being harassed and disoriented by javelin-throwers.

The Role of Numidian Cavalry

Perhaps the most decisive element of Scipio's strategy was his alliance with Masinissa. The Numidian cavalry, led by Masinissa himself, was crucial in outmanoeuvring Hannibal's mounted forces. In previous battles, Hannibal's cavalry had been his ace in the hole, dominating the flanks and enveloping Roman armies. But at Zama, the tables turned. The Numidian cavalry not only held their ground but also routed Hannibal's horsemen, leaving the Carthaginian flanks exposed.

The Final Blow

As the battle raged, Scipio's troops maintained their discipline, executing his plan with precision. When Hannibal's elephants failed to break the Roman lines, the balance shifted. Scipio ordered his infantry to advance in a controlled, staggered formation, drawing Hannibal's forces into a trap. At the critical moment, the Numidian cavalry returned to the field, attacking the Carthaginian rear and turning the tide decisively in Rome's favour.

The result was a resounding victory. Hannibal, who had seemed invincible for so long, was finally defeated. Zama wasn't just a military triumph—it was a testament to Scipio's ability to combine preparation, adaptability, and leadership under pressure.

A Leader's Humility

After such a monumental victory, one might expect Scipio to bask in glory, accepting every honour Rome had to offer. Yet, true to his character, Scipio demonstrated remarkable humility. When the Senate and people of Rome sought to grant him excessive titles and privileges, he declined, taking only the honorary title *Africanus* to mark his triumph in Africa.

Why Did Scipio Refuse Excessive Honours?

Scipio understood that Rome's success wasn't his alone—it was the result of collective effort. From his troops to his allies, many had contributed to the victory at Zama. By refusing extravagant accolades, Scipio reinforced the idea that leadership isn't about personal glory; it's about service to a greater cause.

This humility also served a political purpose. Rome valued leaders who upheld Republican ideals over personal ambition. By rejecting excessive honours, Scipio set himself apart from figures like Hannibal or Alexander the Great, whose power often seemed to overshadow their nations. Scipio's restraint preserved his reputation and secured his legacy as a leader who prioritised Rome's stability over his own ego.

Lessons from Zama: Adversity as Opportunity

The Battle of Zama is a masterclass in turning adversity into triumph. Scipio faced an opponent who was, by all accounts, his superior in experience and reputation. Yet, by embracing flexibility and focusing on preparation, he achieved a victory that changed the course of history. Here are the key takeaways:

1. **Adaptability Wins the Day**:

Scipio's ability to adjust his tactics to counter Hannibal's strengths was the foundation of his success. In our own lives, rigid plans often falter when faced with unexpected challenges. The ability to adapt and think creatively is what separates success from failure.

2. **Preparation Builds Confidence**:

Scipio's calm demeanour on the eve of battle wasn't just a natural trait—it was the result of meticulous preparation. By anticipating challenges and training for them, he inspired confidence in his troops and himself. Whether you're preparing for an exam, a job interview, or a personal challenge, thorough preparation is the key to facing the moment with poise.

3. **Success is a Team Effort**:

Scipio's victory wasn't achieved in isolation. His alliances, particularly with Masinissa, played a pivotal role. This reminds us of the importance of building and nurturing relationships that complement our strengths.

4. **Humility Amplifies Leadership**:

By refusing excessive honours, Scipio demonstrated that true leadership isn't about personal gain. Humility not only builds respect but also reinforces the trust and loyalty of those you lead.

Workbook: Turning Adversity into Triumph

To apply the lessons of Zama to your own life, use this workbook to reframe challenges as opportunities for growth.

Step 1: Identify the Adversity

What challenge are you currently facing? Be specific. For example:

- "I'm struggling to meet a major deadline at work."
- "I feel overwhelmed by the complexity of my project."
- "I'm facing stiff competition for a promotion."

Step 2: Analyse the Challenge

Break the problem down into its components:

- What are the specific obstacles?
- What resources or skills do you need to overcome them?
- Are there external factors influencing the situation (e.g., team dynamics, time constraints)?

Step 3: Develop a Flexible Plan

Like Scipio's adaptable strategy at Zama, your plan should account for potential setbacks:

- What's your primary approach to overcoming the challenge?
- What alternatives can you prepare if your initial plan doesn't work?
- Who can you enlist for support or collaboration?

Step 4: Prepare and Practise

- Hone the skills or knowledge needed to tackle the challenge.
- Simulate potential scenarios to build confidence.
- Use visualisation techniques to rehearse success.

Step 5: Reflect and Adapt

After addressing the challenge, evaluate your performance:

- What worked well?
- What could you improve next time?
- How did the experience help you grow?

Closing Thought: Triumph Through Resilience

The Battle of Zama was not just a victory for Rome—it was a triumph of preparation, strategy, and humility. Scipio Africanus turned what could have been an insurmountable challenge into a moment of greatness, proving that even the most formidable obstacles can be overcome with the right mindset.

As you face your own battles, remember Scipio's example. Embrace adversity as an opportunity to grow, prepare meticulously, and lead with humility. Whether your challenge is a personal goal, a professional hurdle, or a life-changing decision, you have the tools to turn the tide in your favour. Like Scipio, your moment of triumph is within reach.

Modern Parallel: Achieving Long-Term Goals After Persistent Effort

Achieving long-term goals often feels like fighting a prolonged battle. The path to success is rarely a straight line; it's marked by setbacks, adjustments, and moments of doubt. Whether you're striving to build a career, cultivate a meaningful relationship, or accomplish a personal milestone, persistence is the force that carries you through the challenges. The journey of Scipio Africanus to his ultimate triumph at Zama mirrors this reality—years of effort, preparation, and resilience led to a single defining moment.

But what does it really take to achieve a long-term goal? It's not just about hard work; it's about staying adaptable, motivated, and focused even when progress seems slow. By reflecting on Scipio's journey and your own experiences, you can unlock valuable insights into how to persevere and succeed.

The Parallel of Persistence

Personal Goals: Small Wins Leading to Big Triumphs

Consider someone training for a marathon. The goal isn't achieved overnight. It begins with short runs, days when motivation wanes, and incremental increases in endurance. Each small victory—running an extra mile, improving pace—builds confidence and brings them closer to the finish line. Similarly, Scipio's capture of New Carthage and his alliances in Africa were steps that paved the way for his victory at Zama. Each success reinforced his momentum, even as challenges arose.

Professional Goals: The Power of Tenacity

In the workplace, long-term goals often require balancing patience with persistence. Imagine an entrepreneur building a start-up. Early days are fraught with challenges—securing funding, gaining customers, refining the product. There are moments when giving up feels tempting. Yet, with each small breakthrough—closing a deal, receiving positive feedback—the vision becomes clearer, and progress accelerates. Like Scipio, who kept refining his strategies and cultivating alliances, the entrepreneur's ability to adapt and persist determines success.

Creative Goals: Overcoming Self-Doubt

For artists, writers, or creators, achieving a long-term goal can feel like a battle against oneself. Self-doubt and fear of failure can creep in, threatening to derail progress. Yet, as with any long-term pursuit, the key lies in breaking the goal into manageable pieces. Writing one chapter at a time or completing one painting leads to gradual mastery. Scipio likely faced his own doubts as a young commander, but he channelled his focus into small victories, each contributing to his overarching vision of defeating Hannibal.

The Role of Reflection in Long-Term Success

Reflection is a powerful tool for staying motivated on the path to a long-term goal. It allows you to celebrate progress, learn from setbacks, and reconnect with your purpose. Scipio likely reflected on his journey often, using past successes to fuel his confidence and past failures to refine his approach.

Take a moment to reflect on your own long-term goals:

- **What have you already achieved?** Acknowledge the milestones you've reached, no matter how small.
- **What challenges have you faced?** Identify how you overcame them and the strengths you discovered in the process.
- **What's your ultimate vision?** Reconnect with why this goal matters to you and how achieving it will affect your life.

Journal Prompt: Overcoming the Odds

Use this journal exercise to reflect on your journey and draw lessons from your experiences.

Step 1: Describe a Challenge You Faced

Think about a time when you overcame the odds to achieve something significant. This could be in any area of life—academics, career, relationships, or personal growth. Write about:

- The situation you were in.
- The obstacles you faced.
- How you felt at the time.

Step 2: Highlight Your Actions

Reflect on the steps you took to overcome the challenge. Consider:

- The specific actions or strategies you used.
- How you stayed motivated during difficult moments.
- Whether you relied on support from others and how that contributed to your success.

Step 3: Identify the Lessons Learned

Write about what this experience taught you:

- What did you learn about your strengths and resilience?
- How did the challenge shape your character or perspective?
- How can these lessons guide you as you pursue your current goals?

Step 4: Connect to Your Present Journey

Think about a long-term goal you're currently working toward:

- How does your past experience inspire you to keep going?
- What challenges might arise, and how will you address them?

- What steps can you take today to move closer to your goal?

Turning Effort into Triumph

Long-term goals often feel overwhelming, especially when the finish line seems distant. But every great achievement is built on a foundation of persistent effort, small victories, and resilience in the face of setbacks. Scipio's journey reminds us that triumph is rarely instantaneous—it's the result of years of preparation and determination.

As you work toward your own goals, remember to celebrate the progress you've made, learn from the challenges you've faced, and stay connected to your purpose. Whether you're climbing a career ladder, nurturing a relationship, or chasing a personal dream, your ability to persist will define your success. Reflect on your journey, take the next step, and trust that each effort brings you closer to your own moment of triumph.

Chapter 9:

Life After Zama – Staying Grounded Amid Success

Victory doesn't always mean an easy road ahead. For Scipio Africanus, the triumph at Zama and the end of the Second Punic War marked the peak of his military career, but it also ushered in a new set of challenges. As he transitioned from the battlefield to the political arena, Scipio discovered that navigating the complex world of Roman politics could be just as treacherous as outmanoeuvring Hannibal. Despite his monumental contributions to Rome, he faced envy, criticism, and opposition from political rivals. His eventual withdrawal from public life offers valuable lessons about the importance of staying true to one's values and finding peace amid external pressures.

The Weight of Victory: Scipio and Roman Politics

After his victory at Zama, Scipio was hailed as a hero. The Roman Senate bestowed upon him the honorary title *Africanus*, a rare and prestigious distinction. For a time, his achievements seemed unassailable—he had delivered Rome from the brink of destruction and secured its position as a dominant power in the Mediterranean. Yet, as often happens with great success, Scipio's rise attracted the envy and resentment of others.

Roman politics, notorious for its infighting and intrigue, proved to be a hostile environment for Scipio. Many senators, particularly those who had opposed his African campaign, sought to undermine him. Some accused him of arrogance, claiming that his popularity threatened the Republic's ideals of shared governance. Others scrutinised his financial dealings, alleging that he had embezzled funds during his campaigns. These accusations were largely unfounded, but they chipped away at Scipio's reputation and placed him under relentless political pressure.

Scipio's experiences reveal the darker side of success: the higher one climbs, the more visible—and vulnerable—they become. His struggles serve as a reminder that even the most celebrated achievements can provoke envy and opposition, particularly from those who feel overshadowed.

Rising Above Petty Disputes

One of the most remarkable aspects of Scipio's post-Zama life was his refusal to engage in petty vendettas. Despite facing baseless accusations and political attacks, he maintained a sense of dignity and composure. Historical accounts suggest that Scipio forgave many of his political enemies, choosing to rise above the fray rather than stoop to their level.

This attitude was consistent with Scipio's broader character. Throughout his life, he demonstrated a focus on the bigger picture, prioritising Rome's welfare over personal ambition. His ability to remain magnanimous, even in the face of unfair treatment, set him apart as a leader who valued principles over politics.

Retreat to Liternum: A Life of Reflection and Peace

As political pressures mounted, Scipio eventually made the difficult decision to withdraw from public life. He retreated to his countryside estate at Liternum, a quiet haven far removed from the chaos of Rome. This move was both practical and symbolic. By stepping away from the political arena, Scipio reclaimed his personal peace, refusing to let his legacy be tarnished by the petty rivalries of the Senate.

At Liternum, Scipio lived a simpler life, surrounded by family and friends. According to tradition, he spent his final years reflecting on his achievements and the lessons of his journey. It is said that he chose to be buried on his estate rather than in Rome, a gesture that underscored his disillusionment with the city's political climate.

Lessons in Sustaining Success

Scipio's life after Zama highlights the challenges of maintaining balance and integrity in the face of external pressures. His experiences offer valuable insights for anyone navigating the complexities of success:

1. Success Attracts Opposition

Scipio's struggles with political rivals illustrate that success often provokes envy. The higher you rise, the more likely you are to face criticism and opposition. While this can be disheartening, it's important to recognise that such challenges are a natural part of any significant achievement.

2. Prioritise Principles Over Politics

Throughout his life, Scipio remained committed to his values, refusing to engage in petty disputes or compromise his integrity. His example reminds us that true leadership isn't about winning every argument—it's about staying true to your principles and focusing on what truly matters.

3. Seek Peace Amid Pressure

Scipio's retreat to Liternum wasn't an act of surrender—it was a deliberate choice to prioritise his well-being and personal peace. In a world that often glorifies constant ambition, his decision serves as a powerful reminder that stepping back can be an act of strength, not weakness.

Finding Your Own Liternum

Scipio's story invites us to reflect on our own lives and the ways we navigate success and its challenges. Consider the following questions:

- **How do you handle criticism or opposition?** Do you let it consume you, or do you rise above it like Scipio?
- **What principles guide your decisions?** Are you staying true to your values, even when under pressure?

- **Where is your Liternum?** What spaces or practices bring you peace and perspective when life becomes overwhelming?

Historical Echoes and Modern Relevance

Scipio's humility and focus on personal peace resonate deeply in today's fast-paced, competitive world. Many people, particularly those in high-pressure careers, face similar challenges—balancing success with integrity, handling criticism, and finding time for reflection.

Whether you're managing a demanding job, pursuing ambitious goals, or dealing with interpersonal conflicts, Scipio's journey offers a timeless lesson: success is not just about achieving great things—it's about sustaining them with grace, balance, and purpose. Like Scipio, we all have the power to choose our battles, forgive our detractors, and retreat when necessary to preserve what matters most.

Closing Thought: The Legacy of a Leader

Scipio Africanus' life after Zama wasn't marked by endless triumphs or unbroken adulation. It was a complex, human story of resilience, humility, and the pursuit of peace. His struggles with politics and his eventual retreat to Liternum remind us that true greatness lies not in the absence of challenges, but in the way we respond to them.

As you navigate your own journey, remember Scipio's example. Embrace success with humility, rise above petty disputes, and never lose sight of your principles. And when the pressures of life become too great, don't be afraid to step back, reflect, and find your own Liternum—a place of clarity, renewal, and peace. In doing so, you honour not just your achievements, but the values that make them meaningful.

Modern Parallel: Staying Humble and Balanced Amid Success

Success can be intoxicating. Achieving your goals—whether personal or professional—often brings a rush of excitement, validation, and new opportunities. But it also comes with its own set of challenges: the pressure to maintain your achievements, the expectations of others, and, sometimes, the envy or criticism of those around you. Handling success without losing your humility or burning out is a delicate balancing act, and it's one that many struggle to master.

Scipio Africanus offers a timeless lesson in navigating success with grace. Despite his monumental victory at Zama and the adulation that followed, he remained grounded, refusing excessive honours and ultimately stepping back when the pressures of politics clashed with his values. His example reminds us that staying true to ourselves, setting boundaries, and practising gratitude are essential for sustaining both our achievements and our well-being.

The Dual Edge of Success

The Thrill and the Burden

On the one hand, success validates our efforts and opens doors to new possibilities. It's a testament to our hard work, talent, and perseverance. But with it comes heightened scrutiny, increased demands, and sometimes a sense of isolation. The more visible our success, the more likely we are to face external pressures—from expectations to envy.

Consider a professional who's climbed the corporate ladder to an executive role. The accomplishment is enormous, but so are the challenges: longer hours, higher stakes, and the weight of being a role model for others. Or think of a writer whose book becomes a bestseller—suddenly, their work is under the microscope, with critics dissecting every word and readers demanding even more.

Success isn't just about reaching a goal; it's about navigating what comes after. Without the right tools, it's easy to lose yourself in the process.

Coping with Criticism and Envy

One of the most difficult aspects of success is dealing with criticism and envy. As Scipio experienced, even the greatest achievements can provoke envy and opposition. His response? Rising above it. He refused to let the opinions of others dictate his sense of self-worth, focusing instead on his values and the broader good.

Practical Tips for Handling Criticism

1. **Separate Constructive Feedback from Negativity**:

Criticism often contains valuable insights—but not always. Learn to distinguish between feedback that helps you grow and negativity that serves no purpose. Take what's useful and let the rest go.

2. **Stay Grounded in Your Values**:

Success can tempt us to compromise our principles to meet others' expectations. Resist this by staying true to what matters most to you, just as Scipio prioritised his integrity over political games.

3. **Don't Engage in Pettiness**:

It's tempting to respond to envy or unfair criticism with defensiveness or retaliation. But rising above such disputes, as Scipio did, preserves your energy and dignity.

The Role of Gratitude in Sustaining Success

One of the most effective ways to stay grounded during times of success is to cultivate gratitude. Studies in positive psychology have shown that practising gratitude improves mental health, strengthens relationships, and fosters resilience. By focusing on what we have, rather than what we lack, gratitude helps us maintain perspective and balance.

The Science of Gratitude

Gratitude activates areas of the brain associated with reward and positive emotion. Regularly practising gratitude has been linked to:

- Reduced stress and anxiety.
- Improved sleep quality.
- Greater overall happiness and life satisfaction.

Gratitude also counteracts the entitlement and ego that can sometimes accompany success, reminding us of the people and circumstances that have supported our journey.

How to Practise Gratitude

- **Daily Reflection**: Spend a few minutes each evening reflecting on the things you're grateful for, whether it's a supportive colleague, a small victory, or even a moment of calm in a busy day.
- **Gratitude Journaling**: Write down three things you're grateful for each day. Over time, this practice trains your mind to focus on the positives, even in challenging times.

Burnout Prevention: Setting Boundaries and Self-Care

Success often brings increased demands on our time and energy, making it easy to overextend ourselves. Without boundaries and self-care, even the most rewarding achievements can lead to burnout.

The Warning Signs of Burnout

- Chronic fatigue and lack of motivation.
- Difficulty concentrating or making decisions.
- Feeling detached or cynical about your work.
- Physical symptoms like headaches or insomnia.

The Importance of Boundaries

Scipio's retreat to Liternum was, in essence, a boundary. By stepping away from the pressures of politics, he protected his peace and prioritised his well-being. In our own lives, setting boundaries might mean:

- Saying no to commitments that stretch us too thin.
- Carving out time for rest and hobbies.
- Limiting access to people or environments that drain our energy.

Self-Care Strategies

1. **Schedule Downtime**: Block out time in your calendar for relaxation and activities that recharge you.
2. **Stay Active**: Physical exercise boosts energy levels and reduces stress.
3. **Connect with Supportive People**: Surround yourself with individuals who uplift and energise you.
4. **Practice Mindfulness**: Techniques like meditation and deep breathing can help you stay present and manage stress.

Practical Workbook: Sustaining Success

Gratitude Journaling Exercise

1. **Goal**: Spend five minutes each day reflecting on what you're grateful for. Focus on three specific things, such as:
   - Relationships (e.g., "I'm grateful for my supportive partner.")
   - Achievements (e.g., "I'm grateful for completing my presentation today.")
   - Personal growth (e.g., "I'm grateful for my improved confidence in public speaking.")

2. **Duration**: Commit to this practice for one week and observe how it affects your mood and perspective.

3. **Reflection**: At the end of the week, review your entries. What patterns emerge? How has this practice influenced your mindset?

Reflect on Boundaries

1. **Identify Stressors**: Write down areas in your life where you feel overcommitted or stretched thin.

2. **Set Limits**: For each stressor, brainstorm one boundary you can implement. For example:

   - If work emails are encroaching on personal time, commit to checking them only during set hours.
   - If social obligations are overwhelming, limit your commitments to one or two events per week.

3. **Enforce Your Boundaries**: Communicate your limits clearly to others, and don't be afraid to reinforce them if necessary.

Closing Thought: Success with Balance

Success is a journey, not a destination. Sustaining it requires more than talent and effort—it demands balance, humility, and self-awareness. By practising gratitude, setting boundaries, and staying true to your values, you can navigate the pressures of success with grace and resilience. Like Scipio, you have the power to rise above criticism, protect your well-being, and focus on what truly matters. Success isn't just about achieving great things; it's about maintaining them while staying grounded in who you are.

Chapter 10:

Becoming Your Own Scipio

Every journey has its lessons, and every hero's story offers inspiration for our own lives. Scipio Africanus' remarkable life wasn't just a tale of battles and triumphs—it was a blueprint for overcoming challenges, achieving greatness, and leaving a legacy. By learning from his adaptability, resilience, leadership, and ability to build alliances, we can navigate our own struggles and victories with greater confidence and purpose.

This final chapter is about taking those lessons and making them your own. Whether you're facing a challenge in your career, relationships, or personal growth, Scipio's strategies offer practical guidance for becoming a stronger, more capable version of yourself.

Recap of Scipio's Core Strategies

1. Adaptability: The Power to Pivot

Scipio's ability to adjust his tactics and mindset was one of his greatest strengths. From countering Hannibal's elephants at Zama to forging alliances in unfamiliar territories, he thrived by embracing change and finding innovative solutions.

Your Takeaway:

Life rarely unfolds as planned. Challenges, setbacks, and unexpected twists are inevitable. Instead of resisting them, channel your inner Scipio:

- **Stay open-minded**: Treat obstacles as opportunities to learn and grow.
- **Think creatively**: Explore unconventional solutions to solve problems.
- **Embrace flexibility**: Be willing to pivot when your original plan isn't working.

2. Resilience: The Strength to Endure

Scipio grew up in the shadow of Hannibal's victories, witnessing Rome's darkest moments. Yet, he didn't let despair defeat him. His resilience allowed him to rally troops, outlast critics, and keep moving forward even when the odds were against him.

Your Takeaway:

Resilience isn't about avoiding failure—it's about bouncing back stronger. In your own life:

- **Cultivate a growth mindset**: View failures as stepping stones to success.
- **Draw strength from adversity**: Use difficult experiences to build emotional toughness.
- **Focus on the long game**: Remember that setbacks are temporary and perseverance pays off.

3. Leadership: Inspiring and Empowering Others

Scipio led by example, earning the loyalty of his soldiers through courage, fairness, and vision. His ability to unite people behind a common goal was crucial to his success.

Your Takeaway:

Leadership isn't about commanding—it's about inspiring. Whether in your workplace, family, or community:

- **Model the behaviour you want to see**: Let your actions set the tone for others.
- **Communicate your vision clearly**: Share your goals and motivate others to work toward them.
- **Empower your team**: Recognise and celebrate the contributions of those around you.

4. Alliances: The Strength of Connections

From his partnership with Masinissa to his ability to win over local leaders in Spain, Scipio understood the value of alliances. He knew that success is rarely a solo endeavour.

Your Takeaway:

Relationships are the foundation of personal and professional success. To build your own alliances:

- **Invest in relationships**: Strengthen connections with people who support and inspire you.
- **Seek out complementary strengths**: Surround yourself with individuals who bring diverse skills and perspectives.
- **Collaborate for mutual benefit**: Approach relationships with a mindset of reciprocity, offering value in return for support.

Applying Scipio's Lessons to Your Daily Life

In Your Career

Scipio's adaptability and leadership offer invaluable lessons for navigating workplace challenges:

- **Facing a new project**? Break it into manageable steps, just as Scipio approached each campaign with clear objectives.
- **Dealing with team dynamics**? Foster collaboration by recognising and leveraging the unique strengths of your colleagues.
- **Pursuing long-term goals**? Stay resilient and focused, even when progress feels slow or setbacks arise.

In Your Relationships

The alliances Scipio built weren't just transactional—they were grounded in trust and mutual respect. Apply this to your own relationships:

- **Strengthen communication**: Be open, honest, and empathetic in your interactions.
- **Prioritise trust**: Show reliability and integrity to build stronger bonds.
- **Value teamwork**: Approach challenges in relationships as a team, working together toward shared solutions.

In Personal Growth

Scipio's resilience and adaptability can also guide your journey of self-improvement:

- **Embrace change**: Push yourself out of your comfort zone and explore new opportunities.
- **Learn from failure**: Reflect on setbacks and use them as lessons for growth.
- **Focus on balance**: Just as Scipio withdrew to Liternum to find peace, prioritise self-care and mental well-being amid life's demands.

Scipio's Lasting Legacy

Even after leaving public life, Scipio's contributions to Rome endured. His victory at Zama wasn't just a military triumph—it secured centuries of stability and growth for the Republic. His leadership inspired future generations, and his name became synonymous with vision, courage, and strategy.

One of the most poignant reflections on Scipio's legacy comes from the poet Virgil, who wrote, "Let others wage war; you, fortunate Rome, will enjoy peace." This sentiment captures the enduring impact of Scipio's victories: they weren't just about winning battles—they were about creating a foundation for lasting prosperity.

As you reflect on Scipio's story, consider your own legacy. What impact do you want to leave on the world? How can you use the lessons from his life to build a life of meaning, purpose, and fulfilment?

Closing Thought: Becoming Your Own Scipio

Scipio Africanus was a man of his time, but his lessons are timeless. His ability to adapt, persevere, lead, and build connections offers a roadmap for overcoming challenges and achieving greatness in any era. As you close this book and step back into your own life, remember that the qualities Scipio embodied are within you as well.

Your battles may not involve war elephants or political intrigue, but they are no less significant. Whether you're striving for success in your career, navigating the complexities of relationships, or pursuing personal growth, you have the tools to emerge victorious. So take inspiration from Scipio's story, embrace the challenges ahead, and start building a legacy of your own. The journey won't always be easy, but as Scipio himself might remind you: the greatest triumphs are worth the effort.

Building Your Narrative: Crafting Your Life Battle Map

Every hero's journey begins with a vision, and yours is no different. Scipio Africanus didn't achieve greatness by chance; he had a clear purpose and a strategy for achieving it. His life was a series of carefully planned campaigns, each building on the last, culminating in his legendary victory at Zama. Similarly, your own journey toward success and fulfilment requires a roadmap—a "life battle map" that outlines your goals, key milestones, and strategies for overcoming obstacles.

This chapter is about taking everything you've learned from Scipio's story and applying it to your own life. It's about recognising that, like Scipio, you have the power to shape your narrative, influence others, and leave a legacy. By creating your life battle map and focusing on your long-term impact, you can turn dreams into reality and challenges into opportunities.

Creating Your Life Battle Map

A life battle map is your personalised strategy for achieving your goals and navigating challenges. It provides clarity, direction, and motivation, much like Scipio's carefully orchestrated campaigns. Here's how to create yours:

1. Define Your Ultimate Vision

Just as Scipio envisioned a victorious Rome, start by defining your own "Zama." What is the ultimate goal you want to achieve? This could be a career aspiration, a personal milestone, or a broader mission. Be specific and ambitious:

- "I want to build a successful business that supports my community."
- "I want to become a published author and inspire others with my stories."
- "I want to cultivate meaningful relationships and live a balanced, fulfilling life."

2. Identify Key Milestones

Break your ultimate goal into smaller, achievable milestones. These are the equivalent of Scipio's early victories in Spain or his alliance with Masinissa—steps that build momentum and bring you closer to your vision. For example:

- If your goal is to launch a business, milestones might include developing a business plan, securing funding, and reaching your first 100 customers.
- If your goal is personal growth, milestones might include learning a new skill, establishing a daily routine, and building stronger relationships.

3. Plan for Challenges

No battle plan survives contact with the enemy, and your life battle map should account for unexpected setbacks. Identify potential obstacles and brainstorm strategies to overcome them:

- What might slow you down? (e.g., lack of time, financial constraints, self-doubt.)
- What resources or support can you rely on? (e.g., mentors, tools, networks.)

4. Embrace Scipio's Principles

Incorporate the lessons from Scipio's life into your strategy:

- **Adaptability**: Be prepared to adjust your plan as circumstances change.
- **Resilience**: Stay committed to your vision, even in the face of setbacks.
- **Leadership**: Inspire and collaborate with others to achieve your goals.
- **Alliances**: Build relationships that support your journey.

Focusing on Long-Term Impact

Scipio's victories weren't just personal triumphs—they reshaped Rome's future, bringing stability and prosperity to generations. Similarly, your successes can have a ripple effect, inspiring and supporting others in ways you might not yet realise. As you pursue your goals, think about their broader impact:

- **Who benefits from your success?** Perhaps it's your family, community, or colleagues.
- **How can you uplift others along the way?** Consider mentoring, sharing your knowledge, or creating opportunities for others.

By focusing on the long-term impact of your efforts, you align your personal journey with a greater purpose, making your achievements even more meaningful.

Reflective Exercise: Write Your Victory Speech

Imagine you've achieved your ultimate goal. You're standing before an audience—friends, family, or colleagues—delivering a victory speech that reflects on your journey. Writing this speech now is a powerful exercise in visualisation and self-belief. Here's how to do it:

Step 1: Set the Scene

Picture the moment of your success. Where are you? Who's with you? What emotions are you feeling? Let your imagination run wild:

- "I'm standing on a stage, holding an award for my contributions to sustainability, with my family cheering in the front row."
- "I'm celebrating the publication of my first book, surrounded by friends at a launch party."

Step 2: Reflect on Your Journey

Write about the challenges you faced, the lessons you learned, and the victories—big and small—that brought you to this moment. Be specific:

- "I overcame self-doubt and rejection to build the confidence I needed to succeed."
- "I learned the importance of patience, adaptability, and surrounding myself with supportive people."

Step 3: Acknowledge Your Allies

Like Scipio's soldiers and allies, the people who support you deserve recognition. Include them in your speech:

- "I couldn't have done this without the mentorship of my teacher and the unwavering encouragement of my friends."
- "To my partner, who believed in me even when I doubted myself—thank you."

Step 4: Share Your Vision for the Future

Conclude your speech with a forward-looking statement that ties your success to a greater purpose:

- "This achievement is just the beginning. I'm committed to using my platform to help others pursue their dreams."
- "My goal is to pay it forward by mentoring the next generation of leaders in my field."

Reflect on Where to Start

The journey to becoming your own Scipio begins with a single step. Take a moment to identify one area of your life where you can start implementing Scipio's principles today. Reflect on these questions:

- **What is one challenge you're currently facing?** How can adaptability or resilience help you navigate it?
- **What is one relationship you can strengthen?** How can building alliances support your goals?
- **What is one small step you can take today toward your ultimate vision?** Whether it's drafting a plan, reaching out to a mentor, or simply reflecting on your goals, every step matters.

Closing Thought: Your Legacy in the Making

Scipio Africanus' legacy wasn't just the victories he achieved—it was the values he embodied and the impact he had on others. As you craft your own life battle map and work toward your goals, remember that your journey is about more than personal success. It's about creating a narrative that inspires, uplifts, and leaves a lasting mark on the world.

So take up the mantle. Face your challenges with Scipio's courage, adaptability, and vision. Write your victory speech, embrace your role as a leader in your own story, and start building a life that reflects your values and aspirations. Your Zama awaits—step forward and claim it.

Conclusion: Your Zama Awaits

Every life has its defining moments. For Scipio Africanus, it was the Battle of Zama—a victory that cemented his place in history and safeguarded the future of Rome. But Zama was more than a battlefield triumph; it was the culmination of years of preparation, resilience, and strategic brilliance. Scipio's journey is a testament to the power of perseverance, adaptability, and leadership—a blueprint for facing life's challenges head-on.

As we close this book, it's time to reflect on what Scipio's story means for your own life. You may not be leading legions into battle or negotiating alliances in foreign lands, but your challenges are no less significant. Whether you're striving for a personal goal, overcoming a career obstacle, or navigating the complexities of relationships, you have your own "Zama" to conquer. And like Scipio, you have the tools to succeed.

Finding Your Zama

Your Zama might be a dream that feels out of reach, a problem that seems insurmountable, or a journey you've been hesitant to begin. It could be:

- **A personal goal**: Training for a marathon, writing a book, or improving your health.
- **A career challenge**: Starting a business, pursuing a promotion, or mastering a difficult skill.
- **A relationship hurdle**: Strengthening connections with loved ones, resolving conflicts, or building new bonds.

Whatever your Zama may be, Scipio's principles can guide you. Start by breaking down the obstacles before you. Identify the small victories that will lead to your ultimate triumph. Build alliances—lean on friends, family, and mentors for support. And prepare for your "battle" with the same meticulous focus Scipio brought to his campaigns.

A Historical Reflection on True Greatness

Scipio's life wasn't just defined by his victories but by what came after. Despite his monumental achievements, he stepped back from public life, choosing peace over power. His retreat to Liternum wasn't an act of defeat—it was a demonstration of humility and wisdom. Scipio understood that true greatness isn't about endless conquest; it's about balance, integrity, and the impact you leave behind.

This aspect of Scipio's story reminds us that success isn't just about achieving goals—it's about sustaining them in a way that aligns with your values. It's about recognising when to fight and when to rest, when to lead and when to let go. In a world that often glorifies relentless ambition, Scipio's humility is a powerful reminder that balance and self-awareness are just as important as victory.

Your Call to Action

The lessons of Scipio's life are timeless, but they're only meaningful if applied. As you close this chapter, take a moment to reflect on your own journey. What is your Zama? What steps can you take today to move closer to your goal?

Start Here:

- **Break Down Obstacles**: Identify the challenges you face and devise a step-by-step plan to tackle them.
- **Build Alliances**: Strengthen your support network and seek out partnerships that can help you succeed.
- **Prepare for Your "Battle"**: Equip yourself with the skills, knowledge, and mindset needed to overcome your challenges.

And remember: The greatest victories often begin with the smallest steps. Every effort you make, no matter how small, brings you closer to your Zama.

Closing Thought: The Greatest Victory

Scipio Africanus didn't just defeat Hannibal—he left a legacy of courage, strategy, and wisdom that continues to inspire. His journey shows us that no obstacle is insurmountable, no challenge beyond our capability. The same resilience and determination that carried him to victory live within you.

As you step into the next chapter of your life, carry these words with you:

"The greatest victory is the one over yourself."

Your Zama awaits. Go forth with courage, prepare with purpose, and conquer with confidence. The best is yet to come.

Ready for Your Next Transformation? Explore More by Rowan X. Adler!

Conquer the World: How to Overcome Insurmountable Obstacles

Discover the timeless lessons of Scipio Africanus and learn how to turn setbacks into opportunities for victory. Packed with ancient wisdom and modern strategies, this book will inspire you to rise above life's challenges and forge your path to greatness.

Rise from the Arena: A Gladiator's Guide to Overcoming Life's Greatest Challenges

Step into the sandals of a Roman gladiator and uncover powerful insights on resilience, discipline, and triumph. This unique blend of storytelling and actionable advice will empower you to face your toughest battles with honour and strength.

Productivity and Time Management

Reclaim your time, master your focus, and design a life you love with this approachable guide. From conquering distractions to building habits that stick, this book is your roadmap to achieving more with ease.

Personal Growth and Self-Improvement

Embark on a journey of self-discovery with this empowering guide to unlocking your potential. Whether you're building resilience, breaking bad habits, or finding clarity, this book will help you take the first steps toward lasting change.

Motivation and Goal Setting

Turn your dreams into reality with practical tools to ignite your motivation and craft achievable goals. This book is perfect for anyone ready to overcome procrastination, build confidence, and stay on track.

Mindfulness Made Simple

Discover how small, mindful changes can lead to big transformations. With relatable stories and step-by-step exercises, this book will help you find peace, focus, and joy in the chaos of everyday life.

Simplify Your Day: Easy Time Management Tips for Success
Learn how to work smarter, not harder, with practical time management tips that fit seamlessly into your busy life. This book is your key to balancing productivity and personal fulfilment.

Explore all of Rowan X. Adler's books and start your next transformation today! Visit www.rowanxadler.com for more inspiration, free resources, and updates on upcoming releases.

✨ Your journey doesn't end here—it's only the beginning. Take the next step today!

www.ingramcontent.com/pod-product-compliance
Lightning Source LLC
LaVergne TN
LVHW010112170826
845678LV00012B/2366

* 9 7 9 8 2 3 0 6 5 7 6 1 3 *